LINKED DATA FOR THE PERPLEXED LIBRARIAN

ALA Editions purchases fund advocacy, awareness, and accreditation programs for library professionals worldwide.

AN ALCTS MONOGRAPH

LINKED DATA
FOR THE
PERPLEXED
LIBRARIAN

SCOTT CARLSON
CORY LAMPERT
DARNELLE MELVIN
AND
ANNE WASHINGTON

ALA Editions
CHICAGO | 2020

Extensive effort has gone into ensuring the reliability of the information
in this book; however, the publisher makes no warranty, express or implied,
with respect to the material contained herein.

ISBNs
978-0-8389-4746-3 (paper)
978-0-8389-4712-8 (PDF)
978-0-8389-4710-4 (ePub)
978-0-8389-4711-1 (Kindle)

Library of Congress Control Number: 2019053975

Cover design by Alejandra Diaz. Text composition by Dianne M. Rooney in the Adobe Caslon Pro
and Archer typefaces.

♾ This paper meets the requirements of ANSI/NISO Z39.48-1992 (Permanence of Paper).

Printed in the United States of America

23 24 22 21 20   5 4 3 2 1

CONTENTS

ACKNOWLEDGMENTS

T he authors would like to thank the members of the GLAM community who generously donated their time to review this work and provide feedback, many of whom graciously agreed to review the text with meager turnaround time: Dorothea Salo, David Mayo, Jeremy Berg, Kate Flynn, Anjanette Schussler, Alena A. McNamara, Jessica Russell, John Fink, Catherine Oliver, and Steven Holloway.

INTRODUCTION

Since the mid-2000s, the greater GLAM (galleries, libraries, archives, and museums) community has proved itself to be a natural facilitator of the idea of linked data—that is, a large collection of datasets on the Internet that is structured so that both humans and computers can understand it. With our specialized needs in discovery, precise searching, authority control, and disambiguation, along with our lengthy history of producing complex, structured metadata, we in the GLAM community could hardly have asked for a better position to be in with regard to the topic. Over the last ten years, our community has published countless articles about experimentation with GLAM linked data; GLAM conferences have gained a reliable presentation topic; the Andrew W. Mellon Foundation provided close to $8 million in funding for a series of linked data collaborations between a group of Ivy League university libraries; and the Library of Congress announced BIBFRAME, a linked data format intended to replace our long-standing MAchine Readable Cataloging (MARC) format.[1] The outcomes of each individual project may vary, but you can't deny that it has been a very exciting decade for linked data in GLAM.

Yet despite this activity, linked data has become something of a punchline in the GLAM community. For some, *linked data* is one of this era's hottest technology buzzwords; but others see it as vaporware, a much-hyped project that will ultimately never come to fruition. The former may be true, but the latter certainly is not. To quote Tim Williams, a proponent of linked data use in the pharmaceutical industry, the rebuttal to the idea that linked data will never happen is the fact that it is, indeed, happening.[2] Google, Facebook, the Wikimedia Foundation, and others are already putting the underlying standards of the Semantic Web to use, often in websites you use on a daily basis (even though you might not know it). Libraries are also part of the wave, with linked data being delivered through the discovery web pages of library service platforms by SirsiDynix, iii Innovative, and EBSCO. Comparing this unfolding reality to the GLAM community's negative perception of it reveals a significant rift, so what's the problem?

First, only a few in the GLAM community use (and evangelize) linked data, compared with the many who do not. Research and experiments in linked library data are costly, in terms of both technological support and staff time spent away from ongoing library work. Visit a GLAM conference's sessions on linked data and you will chiefly find attendees who have the institutional and financial support to play with linked data (not to mention the institutional and financial support to simply attend conferences). The result is a small assemblage of linked data enthusiasts that rarely grows or changes, which in turn stagnates the technical infrastructure that would welcome others into Linked Data Land.

Our failure to grow this audience is only matched by our field's inability to communicate the practical opportunities of linked data to others in the GLAM community. With all due respect to our technically minded kin, not everyone in GLAM Land has the technical background that is implicitly required to understand linked data concepts; likewise, not everyone in the GLAM linked-data community is able or willing to explain those concepts in a nontechnical fashion. When the GLAM community does ask our enthusiasts to slow down and explain the topic of linked data, too often the explainers fall back on technical jargon, an unintentional (or, in some cases, *very* intentional) form of gatekeeping. If the GLAM community cannot adequately communicate linked data principles to its members, then we either don't actually understand the subject or we don't have an interest in effectively communicating it. The result is a pervasive myth that linked data is too complex for nontechnical GLAM audiences to understand.

In response, this book aims to smash that myth into a thousand jagged shards by presenting the basics of linked data. It is written with the perspective of the GLAM community in mind—specifically librarians, and even more specifically, librarians whose background may not be traditionally considered "technical." The politics of such a statement are (quite rightly) a minefield, since members of departments aligned with cataloging, metadata, and patron-focused catalog searches are often disregarded as "technical, but, you know, not *technical*." This book intends to strip away that pretense and present basic information about linked data in a clear, jargon-minimized way.

That being said, due to the nature of its subject matter, this book inevitably becomes increasingly technical as it wears on. For example, chapter 5 includes samples of a linked data search tool called SPARQL, which may appear unintelligible to those without some experience in SQL (Structured Query Language), which is used to interact with data inside relational databases, or programming languages such as Python. The inverse situation is that library staff with a broad technical background may find portions of this book redundant or overly simplistic. And that's okay! If anything, it means you may be more skilled with linked data than you might have thought.

While we're on the subject of experience, please be aware that while this book is a great primer on linked data basics, it is not an exhaustive dive into the topic, nor is it intended to make you an expert. Rather, its purpose is to get you up to speed and conversant on a (relatively) new technology that could jostle libraries (and archives, galleries, and museums) into new cultural and technological territories. Once you've finished this book, if you find yourself still interested, or better yet, energized by the discussion, there are plenty of opportunities to get involved and work on linked library data, with chapter 7 to get you started.

NOTES

1. LD4L, "LD4L: Linked Data for Libraries," www.ld4l.org/.
2. Tim Williams, "Overcoming Resistance to Technology Change: A Linked Data Perspective," PHUSE EU Connect 2018, www.phusewiki.org/docs/Frankfut%20 Connect%202018/TT/Papers/TT01-tt04-19214.pdf.

ENQUIRE WITHIN UPON EVERYTHING
The Origins of Linked Data

The hardest part of being a developer isn't the code,
it's learning that the entire internet is put together
with peanut butter and goblins.

—Sarah Drasner, developer
advocate at Microsoft[1]

C hances are, you are reading (or listening to) this book because you have questions about *linked data*, that prevalent, somewhat inscrutable term that has been buzzing around the GLAM-o-sphere for the better part of a decade. Perhaps you work in a position that doesn't have much of a technical component. Or maybe your job is highly technical, but you still aren't sure what to make of the voluminous conference presentations and webinars on linked data that you've attended. Maybe you're just looking for a refresher. Whatever your background, we welcome you to this book.

In preparing this book, we spoke to countless librarians about what they really wanted to know when they began learning about linked data, and what some of them still want to know. Not surprisingly, the single most recurring answer comes down to: why? Why are we still talking about linked data for libraries when there seems to be so little progress in the field? What makes this metaphorical White Whale of a technology so special? What does it have to do with us?

To be able to answer these questions, we need to tell the short, very recent history of the technologies that power linked data. As it turns out, talking about the history of linked data means also talking about the World Wide Web. In fact, linked data's existence was, and continues to be, inextricably intertwined (or do we mean *linked?*) with the creation of the web, which was the most important invention of the late twentieth century. This chapter covers the chronological footpath between these two technologies, allowing us to understand the *why* of linked data before we attempt to tackle the *how* in the rest of this book.

To do this, we need to jump back a few decades to the 1980s. What we think of today as the Internet did not exist then, but there was a primordial version, born in the 1960s. Contrary to popular belief, the internet was not designed by the U.S. government as a communications backchannel in the event of nuclear war. In fact, the program—the Advanced Research Projects Agency Network (ARPANET), funded in 1966 by the U.S. Department of Defense—was actually an experiment in distributing computing power among geographically separate research institutions; in this way, a facility that needed more processing power than was available on-site could reach out to use someone else's computers. The ARPANET was eventually shut down in 1990, but its side projects—for instance, research on long-distance communication and secure data transfer—effectively brought us closer to what we recognize as today's internet.[2]

By the early 1980s, there was finally a capacity for computers to connect to a network of different networks—the definition of an "internet"—but it was certainly not for everyone. The online interfaces were almost entirely text, which meant that navigating the network required some degree of command-line proficiency. Today, it is comically easy to click a link to read an article online, but in the pre-web days, simply acquiring a text document was a somewhat cumbersome task. Putting aside the knowledge needed to point a file-transfer program at a specific server, the user would have needed to know (1) that the file existed and was available to download; (2) the appropriate log-in and password to access the server; and (3) where on the server (i.e., in what folder) the file was kept. Since the first internet service resembling a search engine did not appear until late 1990, finding stuff online required being on the right electronic discussion lists or accessing Usenet newsgroups (the precursors to modern online forums) at just the right time.[3]

THE WORLD WIDE WEB

Into this background steps the main character of our story. In June 1980, an Englishman named Tim Berners-Lee spent six months as a consultant at CERN, the European Organization for Nuclear Research, known today for operating the largest and most powerful particle collider in the world. (Less renowned but no less awesome was the Cernettes, a long-running doo-wop band of women working at CERN.)[4] The son of computer builders and programmers, Berners-Lee took the consulting job to work on systems that would enable instant data acquisition and distribution. Another project, however, would soon capture his attention.

Historically, CERN has employed vast numbers of people at a time. During Berners-Lee's tenure there, the interlacing job functions, projects, and software needs of thousands of other CERN researchers became too much for him to remember on his own. In response, he created a program designed to store this web of random, associated information. The program—dubbed ENQUIRE after his cherished childhood almanac, *Enquire Within Upon Everything*—was capable of describing documents, people, internal working groups, and other real-world things at CERN using roughly a dozen two-way relationship markers.[5] (Figure 1.1 contains a handful of example diagrams imagining how these objects and relationships might have been described in

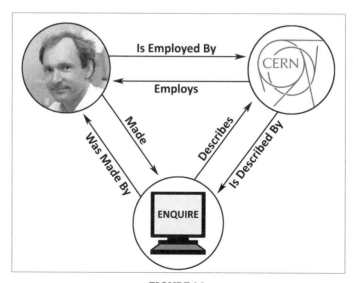

FIGURE 1.1
Enquire example diagram featuring Tim Berners-Lee

ENQUIRE, which now no longer exists.) Berners-Lee would later write that because ENQUIRE stored its information differently than how most people store files in directories today, intuitive leaps from random associations were possible; these connections could then be cross-referenced as new connections with other entities within the ENQUIRE program, automatically connecting back to the original entity.[6]

Part of ENQUIRE's structure was informed by *hypertext*, a term coined by information technology pioneer Ted Nelson as a Harvard graduate student in the early 1960s. Hypertext was a nonlinear, nonsequential form of writing in which sections of text—either whole pages, paragraphs, or short bursts of words—could be connected to text elsewhere, not unlike footnotes. Users reading hypertext on a computer could click these links to follow whichever informational rabbit hole they wanted. Nelson spent most of his professional life pursuing "Project Xanadu," a piece of conceptual software that would use hypertext to facilitate out-of-sequence reading, visualize changes between documents, and source quotations between texts using—wait for it—two-way links running between text and information points. (After more than fifty years in development, Nelson finally delivered a working version of Project Xanadu in 2014.)

His consulting job finished, Berners-Lee left both CERN and ENQUIRE, which was admired by colleagues but not used. He rejoined CERN in 1984, facilitating communication between CERN's computers and networks, and he also resurrected the idea of ENQUIRE. "In addition to keeping track of relationships between all the people, experiments, and machines, I wanted to access different kinds of information, such as a researcher's technical papers, the manuals for different software modules, minutes of meetings, hastily scribbled notes, and so on," he later wrote. "Furthermore, I found myself answering the same questions asked frequently of me by different people. It would be so much easier if everyone could just read my database."[7] But, he soon realized, the last thing he wanted was to create an actual database of information and links, especially one that was centralized. A distributed, decentralized system, on the other hand, could not only scale to the demands of a large number of users, but also guaranteed that anyone could access it without special privileges.

Intrigued by that nascent network-of-networks, Berners-Lee decided to magnify ENQUIRE into a larger system that he could pitch to CERN as a documentation system that would not disrupt his colleagues' organizational styles. The goal was to present information universally to the user, no matter the computing platform. Documents would be written in a standardized way that, upon access, would convey the textual content and structure of a written document, including links to other documents. Without needing to manage a central database of links, adding new documents would be ridiculously easy; anyone could link to anything else, so long as they knew where it was located in the system.

On the advice of his boss, Berners-Lee collected his ideas into a proposal in early 1989, concluding that "a universal linked information system" should be a technical goal for managing information inside and outside of CERN. The proposal read: "The aim would be to allow a place to be found for any information or reference which one felt was important, and a way of finding it afterwards. The result should be sufficiently attractive to use that the information contained would grow past a critical threshold, so that the usefulness of the scheme would in turn encourage its increased use."[8] A collective shrug from the CERN community stalled the project until late 1990, when Robert Cailliau, a Belgian engineer, joined Berners-Lee as a project manager. Cailliau's first task was to hone the proposal and ask for a catchier name. Berners-Lee retitled his project "WorldWideWeb: Proposal for a HyperText Project."[9]

With Cailliau organizing, Berners-Lee was free to get to work on the underlying structure of the web, inventing a suite of protocols and tools allowing the exchange of digital files. The Hypertext Transfer Protocol (HTTP) would allow hypertext documents to be requested and exchanged through transactions with a server, while Uniform Resource Locators (URLs) specified the locations of documents on the server. Finally, the exchanged documents were written in Hypertext Markup Language (HTML), which would be decoded and displayed to the user. Inspired by a preexisting language called Standard General Markup Language (SGML), HTML is built on a standard set of components, the most important of which are tags, or descriptors set between angle brackets. The following, extremely simple example still stands as a working HTML document:

```
<!DOCTYPE html>
<html>
        <head>
                <title>Web page title</title>
        </head>
        <body>
                <p>Hello world!</p>
        </body>
</html>
```

The text between the <head> tags describes basic information about the page we don't see; our example includes a title, but this could also have links to other HTML or text documents with additional information. Meanwhile, the <body> section is the visible content that shows up when we access a web page. Note that the body text of this page—"Hello, world!"—is set within a <p> or paragraph, tag. This tag effectively functions as two different kinds of markup language: first as *descriptive markup*, explicitly describing the text as a unit of human writing; and second, it is also *procedural markup*, instructing the web browser to treat this text as one would display a paragraph in other kinds of human writing.

By the end of 1990, a proto-web was up and running at CERN, featuring a simple, text-based website about the project.[10] As a bigger proof of concept, Berners-Lee and Cailliau converted CERN's massive telephone directory of 10,000 employees to HTML, eliminating the need for print copies.[11] (Berners-Lee also published a web page about the Cernettes, making them the first musical group to have a web page, as well as the subjects of the first-ever photograph published to the web.)[12]

Bolstered by CERN's response, in August 1991, Berners-Lee responded to a message on the alt.hypertext newsgroup, announcing the World Wide Web (WWW) project.[13] From there, CERN began offering its source code to anyone who wanted it and urged people to improve upon their work. In 1992 several physics labs, including the National Center for Supercomputing Applications (NCSA) at the University of Illinois, set up their own web servers; and by January 1993 there were fifty known web servers.[14] After seeing a local demonstration of the web, Marc Andreessen, a bored undergraduate student working at the NCSA, partnered with programmer Eric Bina to work on a web-browsing app that, unlike the software distributed by Berners-Lee and Cailliau, did not require extensive command-line experience to run. Their browser, Mosaic, simplified the process of getting the web onto home computers while adding personal flourishes, including modifying HTML to better handle images and graphics; a year after Mosaic's release in 1993, the number of web servers had rocketed to 1,248.[15] The World Wide Web had begun to ascend with particle-accelerator speed.

THE LIMITS OF HTML

Most of the history books written about the internet end here, often because a good chunk of them was written before the end of the twentieth century. The web has grown rapidly and evolved significantly since its accidental birth in the early 1990s, with much shepherding credited to Berners-Lee; upon leaving CERN in 1994, he founded (and still leads) the World Wide Web Consortium (W3C). The W3C continues to be an international standards organization to improve the quality of the web, periodically updating HTML while endorsing other emerging web standards, such as Extensible Markup Language (XML) and Cascading Style Sheets (CSS). However, we may be forgiven for wondering if, behind the scenes, the success of the web rang hollow with its creator. Indeed, almost none of the relationship aspects from ENQUIRE were brought forward to the World Wide Web, with the exception of hyperlinks between web pages; even then, a link to another page carries no intrinsic significance, except to signify that we expect to safely arrive at another HTML page. For instance, imagine looking at someone's personal website; somewhere in the page, a link is anchored to a piece of text: "Click here to see my sister's online store!" In the World Wide Web as it was designed, the only thing that truly signifies that link as (a) an online store or (b) that it is connected to you through a family relationship is a series of four words—"my sister's online store"—written by an English-speaking human and intended for other English-speaking humans to read it. By itself, the HTML has no way of codifying either piece of information; your link, and thus those two pieces of information, are not understandable to a machine that has no ability to comprehend the concepts of "online store" and "sister." Once that link is clicked, any context about the relationship between those two web pages dissipates like smoke in the atmosphere.

As the web began to swell with HTML content, that kind of contextual information became a necessity. In the early days of the web, there was so little content that the totality of entire regions of web content could be collected, described, and published on a web page like an annotated bibliography. (One such "web directory" from 1992, created by Berners-Lee, listed thirty of the known web servers across the world.)[16] But as the internet took off, the total estimated number of websites jumped to a couple thousand in 1994 and had reached (roughly) 17 million by the turn of the century.[17] (There are now about 1.5 billion websites and, depending on whom you ask, somewhere between

5 and 60 billion web pages.) With no feasible way for humans to manually index and describe millions of HTML documents, internet companies responded by inventing search engines. Search engines deploy web crawlers—automated "bots"—to systematically scour the internet, looking for new and updated web pages. The discovered pages are then consumed by the search engine (a process called *indexing*) and digested into an internal database, where information from the pages is associated with search terms drawn from the information itself. When someone uses a search engine, it examines its indexed content and returns its best guesses as to what the user was looking for. The companies that own major search engines spend quite a lot of money on researching, developing, and sharpening the algorithms that process HTML content, much of which is, again, written by humans for other humans to read. Consequently, those algorithms are highly prized company secrets; after all, while descriptive markup can be part of HTML tags—for example, `<blockquote>` and `<cite>` intuitively describe HTML content as block-quotes and citations, respectively—the value of indexing a web page is in being able to machine-process what its content is actually about. And while the World Wide Web has proven to be extremely handy in connecting documents and displaying them to human users, there were no methods built-in to describe the intrinsic "aboutness" of a web page. The `<head>` tags in a website may identify it as an online music store, but does the algorithm that's indexing the site know what a store is? Or, for that matter, what music is?

Not that people didn't try to fix this. As early as 1995, researchers and developers began working on a `<meta>` tag that "defin[ed] a set of words to use to allow document cataloging."[18] Placed among the other information in the `<head>` tag, meta tags allowed web authors to embed information that was previously undefined in HTML, including keywords and description of the page's content, language, and authors. By 1996, a common standard existed for some `<meta>` tags, but not for including keywords.[19] Nevertheless, a handful of web search engines began supporting and recommending the use of keywords in the `<head>` tag, which could then be used in the retrieval and ranking of web content. Search engines gambled that web developers and companies could be trusted to provide accurate and honest descriptions of their content in exchange for web indexing. Naturally, webmasters quickly figured out that hundreds of unrelated terms and words could be stuffed into the keyword tag in an effort to game the ranking systems. Within a few years, search-engine support for a keyword `<meta>` tag dwindled, meaning that search engines would have to develop their own methods of mechanically parsing the content of web pages to fill up their indexes.

To sum up, for almost twenty years, search engines have relied on increasingly complex machine methods of sifting through billions of web pages, and then used complex algorithmic systems to intuit their meanings from human-created text. Consider that over that same time frame, our use of internet search has evolved from the basic research and navigation of content to relying on the internet to facilitate discourse, record history, and even help us remember basic facts. This vast universe of uses depends on machines being able to divine meaning from things we wrote for other humans in an assortment of written and spoken languages. No wonder the search engine companies keep those processes secret.

ENTER THE SEMANTIC WEB

Less than a decade after the web's creation, Berners-Lee published an abridged autobiography that focused on the development of the web. In it, he envisioned the future of his invention: an extension of the World Wide Web that could be processed, directly or indirectly, by machines. The web, as he saw it, had become dependent on machines to find and understand content that was created primarily for human consumption. "If HTML and the Web made all the online documents look like one huge book," Berners-Lee argued, then this new phase would "make all the data in the world look like one huge database."[20] He laid out a theoretical framework in which data on the web was packaged in a way that could be understood by machines—computers, bots, and other automated processors—just as easily as by humans. He termed this new-phase internet the *Semantic Web*, so named to highlight the expectation of unambiguously crafted data. The old web—the web of documents—was implicit, murky, and unpredictably structured. Data on the Semantic Web would be explicit and structured.

For a moment, consider what you know when you hear the name *Charlie Chaplin*. You may not be a historical expert, but through cultural osmosis, you have probably retained some information about him, such as his persona as "the Little Tramp" and at least one of his professions (an incredibly famous comedic actor, as well as a highly regarded director, writer, and composer). Hard-core fans or film scholars will know much more about him, including the names and release dates of his films, his frequent co-stars and collaborators, and biographical details, such as his childhood spent in a London workhouse, the controversial paternity lawsuit filed against him, allegations of Communist ties, and his de facto expulsion from the United States.

Whether your knowledge about Chaplin is finite or bottomless, your brain already understands certain underlying concepts because it has spent the bulk of your lifetime connecting the dots in the background. In fact, in the process of reading some of these extremely topical details that might be new to you, your brain is adding value and context to your recognition without you knowing it. Without really considering it, you probably

1. have ascertained that Chaplin was a human being who expressed a masculine gender identity;
2. possess a basic understanding of comedy and humor, even if you cannot explicitly explain them other than knowing what "funny" is;
3. understand what movies are, and that actors portray roles in films;
4. know that London is a city in the United Kingdom, which itself is a collection of countries, which are politically defined territories.

And so on and so on. Your brain works very hard, and has for the entirety of your life, to register these concepts and make connections, so that when someone mentions the words *Charlie Chaplin* to you, you recognize the concept of a human male who made movies without your having to manually connect to the concepts of human beings, comedians, filmmakers, and Londoners.

To a computer, *Charlie Chaplin* is a 15-character string (or sequence) of symbols—mostly letters from the Roman alphabet. That particular pattern of symbols represents a series of sounds that are meaningful to humans; these sounds elicit a series of thoughts and concepts in the human brain which help humans recognize and understand, conceptually, what a "Charlie Chaplin" was. But to a computer, the sum total of those symbols is devoid of any larger meaning, other than as a pattern of text symbols that can be used to match other strings of text symbols. The early-to-middle history of internet searching was built, in part, on bots scouring HTML data for words and text strings that could be matched with search queries. Proprietary search algorithms, like Google's, mix in other elements to answer a query, but to a large extent, any page with a high rate of matching text strings becomes a viable internet search result. Under these conditions, web pages about Chaplin the actor-filmmaker become potential matches for search queries about his son, Charles Chaplin Jr.; the French painter Charles Joshua Chaplin; and Richard Patrick Bennett, a Jamaican ragga DJ who adopted the stage name Charlie Chaplin.

As an extension of the existing web, the Semantic Web offers a solution to this situation: the ability to create databases that represent facts, concepts, places, times, and people in a way that a computer can intuitively process. One of these databases could contain a *dataset* (a subset collection of data within a database) with a *node* (a specific, unambiguous entry, otherwise known as a "record" in Library Land) that represents our human being, Charlie Chaplin. Verifiable facts and measurable values about this entry—his dates of birth and death, his occupations, the places where he was born, lived, and died—could be added to this node, distinguishing it from, say, other nodes representing his son or Chaplin the ragga musician.

Of course, a human being rarely exists as an island in space and time; we are always connected, through friendships, bloodlines, geographic locations, events, artistic works, and shared experiences. These connections can enhance and augment our database, binding otherwise disconnected nodes by explicitly stating relationships. Our Chaplin node could be connected to that of his son, Charles Jr., along with his other children, his spouses, and the films he created, which then implicitly present the possibility of connecting Chaplin to his costars and crew members. The unspoken premise here is that one node almost always leads to another, and that one to another, ad infinitum, forming a true web of data. With sufficient connections between each node, a computer could leverage the aggregated knowledge to interpret a data search and deliver a set of results directly related to the actual query subject, rather than hoping to just match a string of text.

CASE IN POINT
Following a Path from Chaplin to James Bond

Figure 1.2 is an example of how even an extremely simple web of connections between nodes of a semantic database potentially offers users a smorgasbord of serendipitous conceptual connections. Starting at the top, our Charlie Chaplin node is explicitly connected to Douglas Fairbanks. Fairbanks, a superstar of swashbuckling movies in the 1910s and 1920s, was a close friend of Chaplin's for much of his life. Fairbanks eventually married Mary Pickford, another superstar of the silent film era, making them an early Hollywood power couple. In 1917 Chaplin, Pickford, and Fairbanks, along with D. W. Griffith, cofounded the United Artists film studio, which released some of their most acclaimed movies of the era, such as Chaplin's *The Gold Rush* and *City Lights*;

Fairbanks's *The Mark of Zorro* and *Robin Hood*; and Pickford's *Sparrows* and *Dorothy Vernon of Haddon Hall*. Through both direct and indirect connections, our Chaplin node allows us to drill through other nodes representing people, events, companies, and films.

But we can go even further than what is pictured in figure 1.2: we can start at Chaplin and end up in a James Bond movie. United Artists still exists a century later, albeit in a slightly different form and as a subsidiary of MGM TV Group and Digital (which is itself a subsidiary of Metro-Goldwyn-Mayer, another of the ancient Hollywood studios). United Artists served as distributor of the 1960s and 1970s James Bond films; it is now co-owner of the copyright and trademarks for the classic James Bond film properties, as well as the sole copyright holder of the rebooted Bond series that began in 2006 with *Casino Royale*. The methods may be convoluted, but in a semantic system with reasonably high-quality metadata, we can follow a clear-cut pathway between three completely different film eras.

However, there is an immediate problem with this idea. According to Berners-Lee, the Semantic Web is "a universal space for anything which can be expressed" using computer-accessible representations and logic.[21] In practice, expressing every conceivable thing in computer-processable terms is a laughably grandiose goal, since it would be subject to standard time and money limitations. Because of real-world limitations, we are more likely to end up with either (a) a collection of unconnected databases encompassing small, highly specific areas of subject matter, or (b) exorbitantly large databases with a shallower level of detail. To be of the greatest possible value, the collections of information on the Semantic Web need to be connected.

In 2006 Berners-Lee put up a personal note on the W3C site, cheekily marked as "imperfect but published." In it, he described his technical vision for "a serious, unbounded web in which one can find [all] kinds of things, just as on the hypertext web we have managed to build."[22] At the time, Berners-Lee was focused on making sure that nodes within a single database shared as many connections as possible; he soon widened his scope to joining disparate datasets together on shared information. He called this idea *linked data*. "Letting your data connect to other people's data is a bit about letting go," he wrote in a 2007 blog post. "It is not about giving to people data which they don't have a right to. . . . It is about getting excited about connections, rather than nervous."[23]

One of the biggest stumbling blocks to understanding linked data is, arguably, the term itself. *Linked data* refers to an ideal scenario in which individual

Figure 1.2
Diagram connecting Charlie Chaplin, Mary Pickford,
Douglas Fairbanks, their films, and United Artists

concepts (nodes) of datasets are connected to other concepts, both inside the dataset and outside in external datasets and databases. The reality, however, is that the vernacular use of the word *link* refers to a URL address, which has led to confusion about linked data in general. Adding URLs to a website does not create linked data; linked data is the result of expressing relationships across the web. In our Chaplin example, we bolster both the completeness of our information, as well as our data's credibility, by taking the time to state that our Chaplin is the same person—the same conceptual entity—that can be found in other datasets. We include specific references to those other database nodes in our example, knowing full well that machines will use the same Semantic Web standards to follow those links and consume their data. We can even tell the machines that our method of linking data—our ability to say that "our thing is the same as this other thing"—can also be described using the same semantic terms that other databases use. It boils down to finding shared relationships between unconnected dots. Just like ENQUIRE did.

At this point, you may be (rightfully) wondering what the history of the World Wide Web has to do with libraries. In the next chapter, we will delve into the current state of library data and try to explain why a still-nascent data format has enraptured a small section of GLAM Land.

NOTES

1. Sarah Drasner (@sarah_edo), Twitter, March 22, 2016, https://twitter.com/sarah_edo/status/712482904090128387.
2. If you are interested in the early history of the primordial internet, there are a few excellent books and resources to draw from: Janet Abbate, *Inventing the Internet* (MIT Press, 2000); Katie Hafner and Matthew Lyon, *Where Wizards Stay Up Late* (Simon & Schuster, 1998); and Ian Peter's website, NetHistory (www.nethistory.info).
3. "The First Search Engine, Archie," last modified September 21, 2002, archived from the original at https://web.archive.org/web/20110719211803/; http://www.isrl.illinois.edu/~chip/projects/timeline/1990archie.htm.
4. The Cernettes, "Cernettes: The Bios," https://cernettes.wixsite.com/cernettes/the-bios.
5. Tim Berners-Lee, "A Brief History of the Web," World Wide Web Consortium, www.w3.org/DesignIssues/TimBook-old/History.html.
6. Tim Berners-Lee, *Weaving the Web* (San Francisco: HarperSanFrancisco, 1999), 10–11.
7. Berners-Lee, *Weaving the Web*, 15.
8. Tim Berners-Lee, "The Original Proposal of the WWW, HTMLized," World Wide Web Consortium, www.w3.org/History/1989/proposal.html.
9. Walter Isaacson, *The Innovators* (New York: Simon & Schuster, 2014), 412–13.
10. CERN has since preserved that first website at http://info.cern.ch/.
11. Johnny Ryan, *A History of the Internet and the Digital Future* (London: Reaktion, 2010), 107.
12. Andrew Hough, "How the First Photo Was Posted on the Web 20 Years Ago," *Telegraph*, July 11, 2012, www.telegraph.co.uk/technology/news/9391110/How-the-first-photo-was-posted-on-the-Web-20-years-ago.html.
13. Isaacson, *The Innovators*, 414.

14. John Naughton, *A Brief History of the Future* (London: Weidenfeld & Nicolson, 1999), 239.

15. Berners-Lee, *Weaving the Web*, 217.

16. Tim Berners-Lee, "World Wide Web Servers," World Wide Web Consortium, www .w3.org/History/19921103-hypertext/hypertext/DataSources/WWW/Servers.html.

17. Internet Live Stats, "Total Number of Websites," last modified August 2019, www .internetlivestats.com/total-number-of-websites/.

18. Davide Musella, "The META Tag of HTML," IETF Tools, last updated December 20, 1995, https://tools.ietf.org/html/draft-musella-html-metatag-01.

19. Danny Sullivan, "Meta Keywords Tag 101: How to 'Legally' Hide Words on Your Pages for Search Engines," Search Engine Land, September 5, 2007, https://searchengineland .com/meta-keywords-tag-101-how-to-legally-hide-words-on-your-pages-for-search -engines-12099.

20. Berners-Lee, *Weaving the Web*, 186.

21. Tim Berners-Lee, "Axioms of Web Architecture," World Wide Web Consortium, last modified August 27, 2009, www.w3.org/DesignIssues/Rules.html.

22. Tim Berners-Lee, "Linked Data: Design Issues," World Wide Web Consortium, last modified June 18, 2009, www.w3.org/DesignIssues/LinkedData.html.

23. Tim Berners-Lee, "Giant Global Graph," Decentralized Information Group, Massachusetts Institute of Technology, last modified November 21, 2007, archived from the original at https://web.archive.org/web/20160713021037/; http://dig.csail.mit.edu/ breadcrumbs/node/215.

UNFUNKY AND OBSOLETE
From MARC to RDF

I magine for a second that you work in a library, archive, or some other GLAM institution's cataloging or technical services department. Members of your institution just delivered a large collection of pristine funk and soul vinyl records, donated to you by a local retired scenester. What's more, some of the administrators have expressed interest in using this collection as a small test project for investigating linked data. Before you can tell them you don't know much, if anything, about linked data, they ask you for some simple diagrams showing the connections between a few of the collection's items before the collection is sent to be processed by your organization's special collections and archives.

What you've been asked to do is a form of *data modeling*; this is the underlying foundation of how human beings have described, recorded, and later encoded data. Your task is to work on sample diagrams that describe the contents of the vinyl collection; these diagrams will inform the *conceptual data model*, the high-level plan that outlines the scope and breadth of your institution's eventual linked-data project; in other words, it's your job to choose the essential pieces of information that will be recorded about each album.

You pick up the first box and thumb through the LPs, finding a collection of first-class grooves: James Brown's *Live at the Apollo*, Stevie Wonder's *Talking Book*, Curtis Mayfield's *Superfly* soundtrack, Sly and the Family Stone's *There's a Riot Goin' On*. The first album in the stack is called *Mothership Connection*, by a band called Parliament. A brief Google search tells you that Parliament was a funk band, led by the songwriter, producer, and bandleader George Clinton (that's him in figure 2.1). Parliament injected pop grooves with outlandish costumes, science-fiction themes, and a mythology of recurring concepts, characters, and themes that strongly influenced Afrofuturism, a cultural aesthetic that explores African American culture in the context of science fiction and techno-culture. The band was (and still is) enormously popular and is considered one of the foremost innovators of funk music. *Mothership Connection* is considered Parliament's masterpiece, and was inducted into the National Recording Registry of the Library of Congress in 2012.

Being a resourceful cataloger, you are fairly sure that an album of this stature has been cataloged, probably many times over. Sure enough, you pull up a solidly cataloged Library of Congress (LC) catalog record of *Mothership Connection*; in fact, the LC record represents the same original vinyl pressing as the copy sitting before you. You sit back and think to yourself: "The work is already done. Why am I making a data model for things that have already been

Figure 2.1
George Clinton, alias Doctor Funkenstein

cataloged and placed into library catalogs?" This chapter is intended to get you to reevaluate the method that libraries have used throughout the twentieth and early twenty-first centuries to describe, store, transfer, and display information about their resources. Which means, of course, we're going to have to talk about the MARC format.

OUR MARC PROBLEM

If you're a part of libraryland, it's fairly difficult to permanently dodge the MARC (MAchine-Readable Cataloging) record. Its data fields, along with their cryptic three-digit identifier codes, represent a half-century of bibliographic data-sharing. And even if you haven't spent a decade in a cataloging-adjacent position, most library and information science degree programs include some kind of introduction to the long-standing bibliographic workhorse that MARC is. More likely, you've attended a conference session, watched a webinar, or read a *Library Journal* article prophesying the imminent death of the MARC record as the library world's primary data format.

In actuality, MARC isn't dying, it isn't broken, and it doesn't need to be fixed. Far from being dead, as of April 2019, OCLC's WorldCat catalog contained close to 450 million bibliographic records from all around the world, which are cataloged in an adapted MARC format. MARC also enjoys a comfortable amount of software support, with parsing tools and programs available in a variety of computer languages and systems for a variety of users. Users proficient in programming languages like Python, Ruby, PHP, and Go can easily find software packages to manage and create MARC data, while Terry Reese's MarcEdit app provides an exhaustive set of MARC tools with a friendly user interface. But above all else, MARC doesn't need to be fixed because it exists and functions exactly as it was created: to provide an electronic version of a card catalog.

Libraries—at least American libraries—controlled their catalogs from the end of the nineteenth century to the late twentieth century through index cards; at first, these were handwritten, but as technology caught up, they became typed and printed. By the mid-twentieth century, some libraries had started creating union catalogs, or printed volumes of their photocopied catalog cards. If these practices sound laborious and unwieldy, especially for large collections . . . well, they were. Little wonder that in the mid-1960s, the Council on Library Resources funded a study of the feasibility of turning catalog cards into data "for the purpose of printing bibliographical products by computer."[1] Early experiments in computer-automated cataloging at the University of Illinois at Chicago, Florida Atlantic University, and the University of Toronto Library showed that the manipulation and retrieval of catalog card information was feasible, but only if the chunks of data were defined and demarcated from each other.[2] In late 1965, the Library of Congress received funding for a pilot project that would distribute its cataloging data to user libraries; this was dubbed MARC. The pilot, as well as the MARC Distribution Service that followed, were directed by Henriette Avram, a computer programmer and systems analyst formerly of the National Security Agency. As chief of the MARC Development Office, Avram is credited with pushing MARC as a bibliographic standard; the MARC structure was adopted as a national standard (ANSI Z39.2) in 1971 and as an international standard (ISO 2709) in 1973.[3]

Whatever we may think of MARC today, it's important to understand just how far ahead of its time it was. Realistically, without MARC, we wouldn't have the integrated library system (ILS) environment, shared cataloging, and bibliographic networking that we have today. But even more than that, with the exception of databases, Avram's creation predates almost every other piece of software in the world that is still in use. By the time MARC was being pushed as a worldwide standard for bibliographic data, AT&T had only just released public versions of its Unix operating system, which became the inspiration and foundation of the Linux, Mac OS, and Android operating systems. Microsoft's MS-DOS, the command-line precursor of Windows, didn't show up until almost a decade later. Consider this for a moment: libraryland's bibliographic data format is older than pretty much all modern computer systems. It is certainly one of the oldest computer data formats, and it may well be the oldest one that is still in active use.

So, if MARC is so great, why are people constantly talking about getting rid of it?

1. MARC Is Cutting-Edge—for 1970

Revolutionary as it may have been, MARC is now simply too long in the tooth. This isn't an assessment born out of ageism; MARC is what the software community calls a "legacy format," a data type that is out of date but still in use. A prime example of MARC's antiquated aspects is the first five characters of a MARC record; in its native form, each record begins with a five-digit number that expresses how long the record is in bytes—or, to put it another way, how many individual letters and numbers make up the record. This is a holdover from the days when MARC files were exchanged physically, via magnetic tape on reels and cartridges. The fact that this record-length data is only five digits means that MARC records are limited to a length of 99,999 characters, a stark anomaly in an age where gigabytes of data can be stored and transferred with ease.[4] Some may question whether such a limitation constitutes a real problem; after all, most MARC records would never need 100,000 characters (that's roughly 15,000 to 20,000 words). But this is just one example, and MARC has many other aspects that are potentially problematic.

2. MARC Tries to Be Too Many Things at Once

In her book *MARC: Its History and Implications*, Avram recounts a 1965 conference at the Library of Congress which concluded, among other things, that "machine-readable record[s] should include all the data presently available on LC's printed card, plus additional information to produce a multipurpose record."[5] The key word in this statement is "multipurpose"; at that same conference, participants' notes indicate a desire for that computerized cataloging format to include "as much data as possible to assure maximum retrieval in the future."[6] MARC hadn't been invented yet, and librarians were still looking to maximize what it could be used for. Today, besides encoding bibliographic data, MARC has been pressed into service as a universal format for bibliographic data in systems, regardless of whether the primary purpose of those systems is storage, transfer, and distribution between ILSs and other systems; manipulation (inputting records, large-scale cleanup, or record normalization); or display (such as in an online public-access catalog, or OPAC). On the surface, this seems like an incredible success story for a format that was meant to print catalog cards. But really, it may be that MARC is being used for too many things at once.

As an example, let's take a look at one of the LC's catalog records for *Mothership Connection*:

The 245 field, the Title Statement, reads as follows:

```
245 10 $a Mothership connection $h [sound recording] /
$c Parliament.
```

The 245 field contains the text of an item's title (subfield a) and a statement of responsibility (subfield c). (Between the two is the GMD, or General Material

Designation, a now-deprecated piece of data indicating that the material is a nonbook format.) Title and author information are essential to bibliographic description; it makes absolute sense to capture the title, as well as the text indicating who created the item, as they appear on the item. But notice that the content of the field appears to form a sentence-like statement; subfield a is capitalized, and subfield c ends with a period—hence the designation *Title Statement*. Why is this information structured like this?

```
000   01368cjm a22003371a 4500
001   12324831
005   20010225135636.0
007   sd bsmenn----e
008   770719s1975 cauzzn
035   __ $a (OCoLC)ocm03126136
010   __ $a 00717929
028   02 $a NBLP 7022 $b Casablanca
050   00 $a Casablanca NBLP 7022 (White House B75)
110   2_ $a Parliament (Musical group) $4 prf
245   10 $a Mothership connection $h [sound recording] / $c
Parliament.
260   __ $a Los Angeles : $b Casablanca, $c p1975.
300   __ $a 1 sound disc (39 min.) : $b analog, 33 1/3 rpm,
stereo. ; $c 12 in.
511   0_ $a Funk songs; performed by Parliament.
505   0_ $a P. funk (Wants to get funked up) --
Mothership connection (Star child) -- Unfunky UFO --
Supergroovalisticprosifunkstication -- Handcuffs -- Give
up the funk (Tear the roof off the sucker) -- Night of the
thumpasorus peoples.
650   _0 $a Funk (Music)
740   02 $a P. funk (Wants to get funked up)
740   02 $a Mothership connection (Star child)
740   02 $a Unfunky UFO.
740   02 $a Supergroovalisticprosifunkstication.
740   02 $a Handcuffs.
740   02 $a Give up the funk (Tear the roof off the sucker)
740   02 $a Night of the thumpasorus peoples.
```

Part of the reason has to do with MARC's origins as a method to automate the printing of catalog cards and physical catalogs. Punctuation was used in card catalogs to separate pieces of information for human eyes. As we mentioned in chapter 1, the human brain is always working behind the scenes, filling in missing information or ignoring what seems inconsistent; punctuation helped structure card data, providing a grounding for a scant set of details being skimmed by human eyes. The other part of the reason has to do with ISBD (International Standard Bibliographic Description), a project created by the International Federation of Library Associations and Institutions (IFLA). ISBD is a set of guidelines for creating bibliographic description as human-readable text. The descriptive rules of the second edition of the *Anglo-American Cataloguing Rules* (AACR2) are based largely on ISBD(G), the General International Standard Bibliographic Description.[7] Although librarians typically separate content standards like AACR2 and Resource Description and Access (RDA) from MARC, ISBD punctuation became more elaborate in library cataloging rules, which inevitably made it common in MARC data.[8] The title statement in our *Mothership Connection* record reflects the intersection of tradition, modern cataloging rules, and data encoding.

So why is our information *still* structured like this? There's nothing wrong with an information standard being presented or displayed with a preference toward human-readability; the question is, why do we extend that preference all the way to our data-encoding standard, to the point that an errant or missing period can prevent a MARC record from being validated? The data elements contained within our *Mothership Connection* 245 field are really just two strings of text—a title and a creator statement—sandwiching a piece of data identifying what kind of item it is (a sound recording). A computer—for example, an OPAC generated by an ILS—can easily put these chunks into the sentence format suggested by the content standard. In fact, some ILSs already do this: punctuation is stripped out of MARC data and manipulated within the OPAC for a custom display. Simultaneously, a cataloging interface could very easily take separated title and author data and construct them into the 245 structure as a preview of how the data would look displayed in an OPAC. There is no realistic need for this data to exist as a sentence when it's being entered or stored.

3. MARC Relies on Human-Readable Text as Data

If you've watched a webinar, participated in a conference session, or read an article on the future of library catalog data in the past ten years, you may have heard the aphoristic slogan "Things, Not Strings." This is a critique of the reliance on free-form, human-readable text in our data—and specifically, MARC data. But for a lot of library people, the slogan is bewildering. Much of our catalog data is written by humans and consumed using human eyes, so why are strings of text such a problem?

The simplest answer is that humans are *not* the primary consumers of catalog data: *computers* are, and not even by a close margin. Broadly speaking, library data has lived in an almost purely digital ecosystem for about fifteen years. True, humans catalog things, and human eyes may be the intended target for such data, but everything that happens in between those two points is some kind of computer-based processing. And as we mentioned in chapter 1, human-intended text has no inherent meaning to the computers that process it.

At their most elemental, computers use a number of basic mechanisms (calculating, matching patterns, and so on) to process data—that is, they check our data for certain conditions and report back when something meets those conditions. Many of these data checks are simply True/False statements (called "booleans" in computer science); if your data is granular enough and you've precisely defined what you're looking for, data processing can yield results with (relative) precision. MARC has several fields devoted exclusively to such computer-processing purposes; these "control fields" often contain a set number of characters, each of which has a predetermined set of values that represents something meaningful to humans. For example, each of the characters in the Physical Description Fixed Field (007) represents a physical characteristic about nonbook items. We could tell a computer to process a collection of MARC records looking for 007 fields coded with specific characteristics unique to items that are vinyl LPs. Our specifications for the computer might look something like this:

```
IF 007 EXISTS IN record AND
007[00] = s AND // 'Sound recording'
007[01] = d AND // 'Sound disc'
007[03] = (b or c) AND // '33 1/3 rpm' or '45 rpm'
007[05] = m AND // 'Microgroove'
007[06] = e:  // '12 in. diameter'
     PRINT record
ELSE:
PASS
```

The computer doesn't care that a "d" in the second character position of the 007 field represents "Sound disc," nor does it know what a vinyl LP is. The computer's job is to loop through each MARC record and see if these characters match the specifications we gave it. If it does, it reports a match; if it doesn't, it moves on. In fact, the characters used in these control fields are meaningless to *us* as well; they're simply stand-ins for other pieces of information that we defined ahead of time.

As our data moves from those stand-ins to strings of text, our ability to produce precise results steadily declines. Part of the reason for this is because the human brain, unlike a computer, is busy working behind the scenes to decode as we listen, read, or otherwise comprehend language, and encode through speech, writing, or some other kind of expression. *Syntactic interpretation*, for example, deals with the construction of a sentence through word arrangement. Millions of unique, full-sentence notes can be found in the 5XX fields of our MARC bibliographic data; each 5XX note can (theoretically) be expressed in an infinite number of ways. Since computer processing is essentially a search for pattern-matching, our syntactic choices mean that none of these notes can be *parsed* (examined) like one of the control fields. On another level, those 5XX notes carry meanings unique to the understanding of the catalogers who wrote them. Divining meaning from an expressed language—or *semantic interpretation*—is an equally ambiguous process, usually requiring interpretation by another human. A patron looking for a book on funk music that also contains discographies is in for a rough search; that sort of information *could* be found in the 504 (Bibliography, Etc. Note) field, but what if the cataloger doesn't consider discographies to be part of the structural or philosophical categories defining bibliographies and indexes? Or what if the cataloger chose to mention discographies, but prefers an alternate term? Could we guarantee that all catalogers would agree on using the term "discography" instead of an "index" or "catalog" of music?

It gets worse when our content standards play fast and loose with the standard for recording such textual information. For some reason, when we record International Standard Book Numbers (ISBNs) in MARC's 020 field, we've been appending human text to indicate which book form they correspond to:

```
020 $a 9781476751078 (hardcover : alk. paper)

020 $a 9781476751085 (pbk. : alk. paper)
```

Ideally, this information should be relegated to a separate field—in fact, LC's documentation for the 020 field directs catalogers to place "statement[s] of qualifying information" into a subfield q, because it's generally considered bad data practice to mix an all-numeric identifier with human-readable text.[9] Yet this information is almost never entered that way; and to make matters worse, our content guidelines provide no relevant guidelines on exactly *how* to textually record such information. Back in 2011, Bill Dueber, a programmer at the University of Michigan University Library, investigated the parenthetical text appended to the ISBNs in his library's catalog. He found over 1.5 million notes made up of more than 13,000 unique text strings, the bulk of them describing either the hardcover or paperback nature of items; at least 90 of those unique strings began with the letter "h": *hard back, hard book, hard bound, hardcover, hard-back, hard-back cased, hardcover-alk. paper* . . . The list goes on.[10] Keep in mind, this information is not stored anywhere else in the record; if we wanted a computer to process binding information, we would first need to parse those thousands upon thousands of strings to find all of the variations of the book binding descriptions we wanted to look for.

Toleration of data inconsistency makes even less sense when the human-readable text is supposed to be a term from a controlled vocabulary. Recall that our *Mothership Connection* 245 data includes the GMD, a now-defunct method of denoting nonbook items in MARC records using a subfield h. After libraries implemented the RDA content standard, the GMD was replaced by three fields—336, 337, and 338—that are intended to separate an item's respective content, medium, and physical carrier forms. The previous 245 data:

```
245 10 $a Mothership connection $h [sound recording] /
$c Parliament.
```

. . . is replaced with:

```
245 10 $a Mothership connection / $c Parliament.

.  .  .

336 ## $a performed music $2 rdacontent
337 ## $a audio $2 rdamedia
338 ## $a audio disc $2 rdacarrier
```

On the one hand, this change represents a step forward for MARC; the content (336) and medium (337) fields make explicit certain characteristics that are only implied by terming this item a "sound recording." But as it happens, the physical carrier data (338) is not only partially duplicate information, it duplicates MARC data in two different places: the physical description (300) field containing human-readable text:

```
300 ## $a 1 sound disc (39 min.) : $b analog, 33 1/3
rpm, stereo. ; $c 12 in.
```

... and the control fields previously mentioned, including the 007 field and the Leader (000 field). Here we have an instance where the physical and content characteristics are represented in three forms: human-readable free text; computer codes; and a controlled term in human-readable text. Of course, much like the fixed field data; the architects of RDA never meant for this information to be displayed publicly; rather, it was an acknowledgment that OPACs and other web-based displays of MARC data might be better suited using this textual information to filter search results. Unfortunately, in this particular case, the 338 term from the LC and RDA's controlled list of terms is "audio disc," a misleading carrier type that could apply to vinyl LPs, CDs, and a host of other obsolescent audio technologies. But under RDA-defined content description, a cataloger could just as well choose another, more meaningful term that is not present in the LC/RDA list of terms, even if this term muddies the information present in the fixed and description fields.

4. MARC Has Difficulty Expressing Complex Relationships

While we're on the subject of meaningful, controlled terms, let's talk about how they relate to the relationships inherent in bibliographic data. The foundations of modern bibliographic description—set up in card-cataloging practices and effectively codified in AACR—were based on describing an item "in hand," rather than gathering information from alternative sources. One of the effects this had was structuring the modern library catalog as a sea of island records; our records share the same data format, descriptive rules, and controlled vocabularies, but outside of these similarities, MARC is mostly unable to describe or communicate the complex relationships between resources, as well as the concepts, people, and places described within them. In the context of card catalogs, this made a certain amount of sense; after all, the real estate of an index card was limited to just a handful of pieces of information. But as our ability to store and retrieve data grew, our methods never changed, leaving us unable to express meaningful relationships in our catalogs. For instance, the Library of Congress currently has two copies of the *Mothership Connection* album: one representing the original LP (LCCN 00717929), and another representing a CD re-release (LCCN 2007576772). There are inherent relationships between these two items: one is an initial release, and the other is a re-release; both of them represent the same creative work; and so on. Sure, we can try to codify these relationships in MARC; fields 760 through 787 are set aside for "Linking Entries" data, which includes "Additional Physical Form Entry" (field 776). On the record of the LP version, we could add the following information:

```
776 08 $i Also issued as: $t Mothership connection $h
audio disc ; 4 3/4 in. $w (DLC)sc#2007576772#
```

The overall purpose of the 776 field is to link "another available physical form of the target item," but once again, the heavy lifting of communication is being done by text intended for humans: the phrase "also issued as" means nothing to a computer, as does the subfield-h designation "audio disc."[11] Furthermore, the CD could conceivably contain the same "also issued as" note in a link to the LP version. In short, the field doesn't actually build a bridge between distinct catalog records; we might be able to write notes to each other describing their relationship, but once again, by storing them as vague text statements, we lock that information out of the reach of computer processing.

The MARC authority format is similarly lacking in relational communication. The LC name authority heading for Parliament is partially summarized in figure 2.2.[12] Parliament's authority record is connected to two of its band

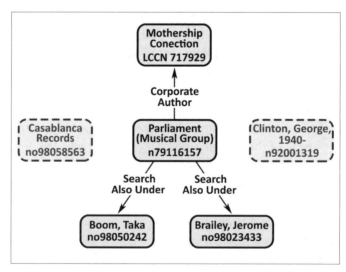

Figure 2.2
**Diagram of Library of Congress name authority
representing "Parliament"**

members, vocalist Taka Boom and drummer Jerome Brailey, both of whom performed on *Mothership Connection*. These connections are made via a reference to Parliament's authority heading in the performers' MARC authority 510 fields (See Also From Tracing -- Corporate Name). Unfortunately, the connections between these personal name records and Parliament's record are devoid of any context of how Boom and Brailey are connected to the band; instead, each has—what else?—a textual note:

```
510 2 $w r $i Corporate body: $a Parliament (Musical
group)
```

The "r" code in the subfield w indicates that the relationship between Taka Boom/Jerome Brailey and Parliament (Musical group) is found in the subfield-i data: "corporate body." One could (correctly) argue that the poor choice of relationship designator is largely due to the actions of the person or persons who cataloged (and thus linked) these records. Still, even if the cataloger(s) had chosen a better descriptor, it would still be a piece of text intended for humans.

5. Outside of Libraries, No One Speaks MARC

Earlier, we discussed the history of the World Wide Web, a technology that has shaped the world in dramatic and pervasive ways. You may have noticed that in telling that story, we left libraries almost completely out of the picture. The internet has, without question, fundamentally changed the landscape of libraries, putting e-books, databases, virtual reference, and web-based OPACs into the hands of eager patrons. But as far as bibliographic data is concerned, there is little intersection with the creation of the World Wide Web. Yes, we now have subfields for URLs, and yes, it is somewhat easier to catalog an electronic resource than it was 15 or 20 years ago. That being said, MARC has remained largely the same as it has for several decades, and that format is mostly incompatible with the internet.

For better or worse, the internet (mostly) runs our lives now. In 2018, more people in North America subscribed to Netflix than to conventional cable and satellite TV.[13] Amazon, a single company, accounts for 5 percent of America's entire retail economy, with an estimated 51 percent of all U.S. households subscribing to Amazon Prime.[14] Locally, increasing amounts of library work—if not the majority of it—require computers and an active connection to the internet. None of these developments should be a surprise, and yet even though this is life now, the internet at large still can't natively deal with our bibliographic data. And though MARC enjoys a decent amount of open-source software support, it remains a large enough pain in the ass for hobbyists, publishers, vendors, and otherwise sympathetic tech people to ignore it, or leave it to us to clean up their attempts. (No joke: Since late 2010, *Wikipedia*'s article on MARC carries a warning that it "may be too technical for most readers to understand."[15] It's probably not a good sign if we can't explain our own format to nonlibrary people.)

When the topics of bibliographic data and the internet come up within library discussions, it's usually within the context of strategizing how to get our MARC data consumed by search engine crawlers, thereby increasing the findability of our collections. Being able to translate our data, or somehow make it more palatable, for the crawlers that scour the web is a worthwhile effort, but it shouldn't be our target result. For one, it prioritizes the conversion of existing data without necessarily reshaping our bibliographic description methods; if all we cared about was feeding Google's crawlers, there would be no need to replace MARC and we could happily keep on generating MARC records for humans to read. Setting aside the fact that Google and Microsoft will happily take our data while giving us absolutely no guarantee that they will actually use it, sticking with MARC does nothing to help make our data part of a burgeoning web of connected data. By reshaping our practices to incorporate the existing web, we not only give ourselves a fighting chance to make sure our data stays relevant and useful, but we become masters of our own destiny, instead of handing off our processes to technologists or corporations that think they know our needs better than we do.

So library data needs to change. Where do we go now? Enter the foundation of linked data and an interesting possibility for the future of bibliographic data: RDF.

RESOURCE DESCRIPTION FRAMEWORK

The Resource Description Framework (RDF) was created in the late 1990s and adopted as a W3C recommendation in 1999. It is the underlying structure of the Semantic Web and, consequently, of linked data. RDF grew concurrently with a special kind of database design: the graph database. In mathematics, a *graph* is an arrangement of things that are, in some form, "related." Recall that in chapter 1, we referred to *nodes* as specific, unambiguous things in a dataset.

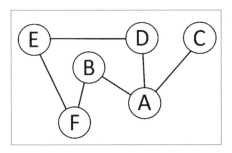

FIGURE 2.3

An extremely basic graph diagram

A graph typically shows a collection of nodes connected to each other, indicating some kind of relationship. Figure 2.3 portrays an extremely basic graph with six nodes (A through F) and some kind of relationship between them.

We do not know what the nodes represent or exactly how they are related to each other, but we can still tell a few important things from the graph. First, we can assume that these nodes are all the same broad kind of "thing," since all of them are represented with the same shape. Second, and possibly more important, the graph is free of a hierarchy; the diagram implies that no single node has any intrinsic importance over another.

RDF shares some of these graph database qualities, especially the expression of relationships free of hierarchy. Foundationally, RDF is a model that says knowledge can be represented in declarative *statements* about *resources*. What is a resource? Anything in the world, according to the RDF concept specification: "physical things, documents, abstract concepts, numbers, and strings [of text]."[16] These statements are stored in a kind of graph database called a triplestore, which gets its name from the statements made in RDF, which are called *triples*. A statement in RDF is like a simple English sentence: it contains a subject, a predicate/verb, and an object, in that order. The Subject-Predicate-Object components of RDF triples are the atomic-level particles of semantic data, and enable us to represent knowledge in a format that can be queried and analyzed by computers. Using what little information we know about Parliament and *Mothership Connection*, we can begin to construct such simple declarative statements in the RDF syntax:

SUBJECT	PREDICATE	OBJECT
Parliament	made	*Mothership Connection.*
George Clinton	is a member of	Parliament.

As a rule, an RDF triple always represents a fact. Earlier, we stated that Parliament was, and still is, an enormously popular and influential band, and that *Mothership Connection* is their masterpiece; even if we bolster our assessments of their popularity and influence with credible evidence, these are still value judgments, and are thus unsuitable to be represented with triples. For example, earlier we noted that *Mothership Connection* was chosen as part of the Library of Congress's National Recording Registry in 2012. The album's inclusion on this list is a fact—that is, we can verify with evidence that it happened—representing a potential triple:

SUBJECT	PREDICATE	OBJECT
Mothership Connection	is part of	National Recording Registry.

Nevertheless, humans can still infer value judgments about entities through triples. Whether or not being a part of the National Recording Registry is anything of value is for us as humans to decide; computers only need to process whether or not the album is a part of the Registry. Also, implicit in this discussion is that a triple not only represents a fact, but a *single* fact; we can connect *Mothership Connection* to more places of recognition than just LC's National Recording Registry, but to do so, we need multiple triple statements.

Figure 2.4 shows some of our previous MARC examples—the *Mothership Connection* record and its related authority data for Parliament and George Clinton—reformatted as (a handful of) RDF triples. The LC's MARC record for *Mothership* is connected to the Parliament authority record simply by containing the text string "Parliament (Musical group)" in the 110 (Main Entry—Corporate Name) field. In figure 2.4, both *Mothership Connection* and Parliament are represented by distinct graph nodes with an explicit relationship between them, expressing Parliament as its creator. Meanwhile, an authority record for George Clinton also exists, but it is connected to neither Parliament nor *Mothership Connection*; here, we can also explicitly connect a node representing Clinton, which is linked to both of our other nodes.

What is there to gain practically from a data model like this? For a start, we're explicitly declaring how three nodes—in this case, three real-world things—relate to each other, creating connections that weren't present in our MARC data. But on a deeper level, RDF is making a statement on how we can define such real-life objects, people, and so on as data. Recall that in our discussions of MARC, implicit was the fact that each field represents a different aspect of bibliographic description. Drill down further and each of those fields has subfields, which represent different pieces of information, depending on which field they belong to. These field definitions, along with their unique rules of entry and syntax, are the main reason why the rest of the world finds MARC

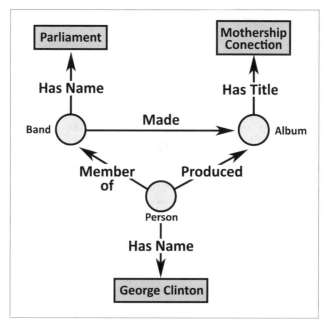

FIGURE 2.4
Mothership Connection, Parliament,
and George Clinton as RDF

so inscrutable: its schema, or the blueprint of how MARC is constructed, is extremely complicated and requires advanced knowledge to use and make sense of. Each of our triples, on the other hand, follows the same syntax: *subject, predicate, object.* This, according to some, is the genius of the RDF specification: since every RDF triple statement consists of a *subject-predicate-object* construction, it is effectively schema-neutral. We can choose whatever data format we want to store or transmit an RDF triple over the web, because they all follow the same underlying concept of resource description through statements. (Chapter 3 deals with some of the popular data formats for RDF triples.)

Also worth noting is that our depiction of figure 2.4 divides its data points into squares and circles. The circles represent the individual nodes being described. Squares, on the other hand, represent information about the nodes that would be transcribed or recorded. In linked data, these are referred to as *literals.* Some literals are measured values, like the album's running time or the year it was released; other literals are identifying information, like *Mothership Connection*'s catalog number and its title. In essence, RDF reduces everything in the world that is knowable, or has existed, into either a thing or a thing's label; this separates the identity of a thing from strings of text, allowing us to represent people, concepts, and places without relying on a string of human-intended text.

And if everything is either a thing or a thing's label, then just about anything, inside and outside of the bibliographic data sphere, can be described and connected to something else. Figure 2.5 puts this into practice, constructing an RDF graph that expands on figure 2.4 by adding nodes for Casablanca Records, Jerome Brailey, and Taka Boom. Notice that there are no overlaps in this model, nor does it suffer from ambiguity; each piece of information is atomized and placed into its own slot, carefully set apart from all the other atoms of data, using the same triple syntax.

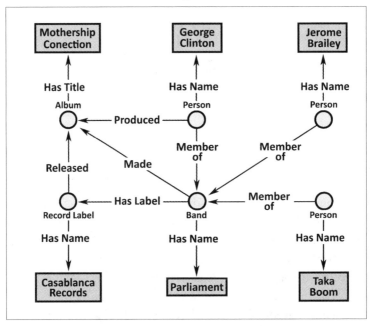

FIGURE 2.5
Mothership Connection, Parliament, and
George Clinton as Expanded RDF

DEEP DIVE
Songs as Entities

Figures 2.4 and 2.5 show real-world nodes connected to a single album. But what about conceptual entities? As an album, *Mothership Connection* is a collection of songs. Songs can exist as both recorded sound and as written notation, but at a higher level, songs are conceptual, artistic works. In the case of *Mothership Connection*, they are intrinsic to the album's overall identity; connecting them as nodes to the album in RDF would make a lot of sense.

Such an approach differs mightily from the LC's MARC record, where the songs are included as a long string of text (in the 505 Formatted Contents Note field) as well as individual entries in 740 (Uncontrolled Related/Analytical Title) fields. Including the songs as 740 fields does give the album extra points of access in an OPAC; most library systems can be customized to treat these 740 entries as they would other kinds of title data, allowing patrons to search and browse for them. However, at the end of the day, these songs are still just strings of text in a notes field, and adding them as 740 fields will give patrons no contextual information indicating that "Unfunky UFO" or "Night of the Thumpasorus Peoples" are parts of an album, let alone that they designate songs at all.

Figure 2.6 shows a sample RDF diagram depicting "Unfunky UFO" or "Night of the Thumpasorus Peoples" as songs connected to *Mothership Connection*. Having this framework in place opens the door to even more triples being connected, such as band members being linked to songs as songwriters, contributing to an even more complete description of the album.

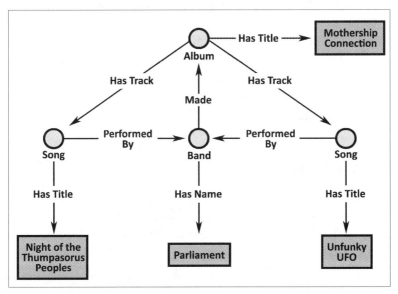

FIGURE 2.6

Songs from *Mothership Connection* as RDF

Already we can feel the psychic turbulence of the librarians reading this example model and asking themselves, "Where do they expect all this extra metadata to come from?" And yes, you are right: the RDF examples in this chapter wantonly use information not contained in the original LC MARC records. We acknowledge that a different library data model would necessitate more metadata. At the same time, library data is, by and large, *already* incredibly detailed and rich. If libraries eventually adopt an RDF-based format for information description, we won't be starting from scratch. We also wouldn't be striking out on our own; the structure of RDF allows different datasets to be integrated into a single graph, even if they were produced by independent, disparate sources. This not only brings us closer to making library-centric data part of a wider, global network of linked data, but it may also reduce some of the inherent redundancy of library work. If computer parsing of linked data can handle the basic data generated by cataloging, then technical services departments as a whole will be able to spend their time making new connections and creating new bibliographic data points, rather than transcribing item information and fixing MARC records.

But before any of that can happen, we first have to atomize our bibliographic data, breaking down everything in our part of the digital world into the smallest relationships and literals we can. We don't have to do these things simply because RDF is newer and shinier than our current state of bibliographic data. We have to do these things because the world we live in runs on the World Wide Web, search engines, and faceted browsing. We have to do these things because the blood that pumps through the veins of the world we live in now consists of data processed by computers. We have to do these things because we need to be a part of the world.

ACKNOWLEDGMENTS

The authors wish to acknowledge the following people, whose work and writing significantly influenced this chapter: Dorothea Salo,[17] Angela Kroeger,[18] Michele Seikel and Thomas Steele,[19] Thomas Meehan,[20] and Ruben Verborgh and Seth van Hooland.[21]

NOTES

1. Henriette D. Avram, *MARC: Its History and Implications* (Washington, DC: Library of Congress Development Office, 1975), 6.
2. Avram, *MARC: Its History and Implications*, 76–78.
3. Ling-yuh W. Pattie, "Henriette Davidson Avram, the Great Legacy," *Cataloging & Classification Quarterly* 25, no. 2-3 (1998): 69.
4. Ruth Holloway, "3 Open Source Code Libraries to Handle MARC-Formatted Records," OpenSource.com, last modified April 21, 2017, https://opensource.com/article/17/4/bit-about-marc-handlers.
5. Avram, *MARC: Its History and Implications*, 6.
6. Karen M. Spicher, "The Development of the MARC Format," *Cataloging & Classification Quarterly* 21, no. 3-4 (1996): 80.
7. *Anglo-American Cataloguing Rules*, 2nd ed. (Chicago: American Library Association, 1978), paragraph 0.22.
8. Library of Congress, Network Development and MARC Standards Office, "MARC Discussion Paper No. 2010-DP01," last modified December 21, 2010, www.loc.gov/marc/marbi/2010/2010-dp01.html.
9. Library of Congress, Network Development and MARC Standards Office, "020: International Standard Book Number," last modified September 24, 2013, www.loc.gov/marc/bibliographic/bd020.html.
10. Bill Dueber, "ISBN Parenthetical Notes: Bad MARC Data #1," Robot Librarian, last modified April 2011, http://robotlibrarian.billdueber.com/2011/04/isbn-parenthetical-notes-bad-marc-data-1/.
11. Library of Congress, Network Development and MARC Standards Office, "776: Additional Physical Form Entry," last modified May 17, 2017, www.loc.gov/marc/bibliographic/bd776.html.
12. Available at https://lccn.loc.gov/n79116157.
13. PricewaterhouseCoopers, "A New Video World Order: What Motivates Consumers?" www.pwc.com/us/en/services/consulting/library/consumer-intelligence-series/video-consumer-motivations.html.
14. Ingrid Lunden, "Amazon's Share of the U.S. E-Commerce Market Is Now 49%, or 5% of All Retail Spend," Techcrunch, last modified July 13, 2018, https://techcrunch.com/2018/07/13/amazons-share-of-the-us-e-commerce-market-is-now-49-or-5-of-all-retail-spend/; Louis Columbus, "10 Charts That Will Change Your Perspective of Amazon Prime's Growth," *Forbes*, last modified March 4, 2018, www.forbes.com/sites/louiscolumbus/2018/03/04/10-charts-that-will-change-your-perspective-of-amazon-primes-growth/.
15. *Wikipedia*, "MARC Standards," last modified July 18, 2019, https://en.wikipedia.org/wiki/MARC_standards.
16. World Wide Web Consortium, "RDF 1.1 Concepts and Abstract Syntax," last modified February 25, 2014, www.w3.org/TR/rdf11-concepts/.
17. Dorothea Salo, "Quia Faciendum Est," Speaker Deck, last modified October 23, 2015, https://speakerdeck.com/dsalo/quia-faciendum-est-with-notes.

18. Angela Kroeger, "The Road to BIBFRAME: The Evolution of the Idea of Bibliographic Transition into a Post-MARC Future," *Cataloging & Classification Quarterly* 51, no. 8 (2013): 873–90.
19. Michele Seikel and Thomas Steele, "How MARC Has Changed: The History of the Format and Its Forthcoming Relationship to RDA," *Technical Services Quarterly* 28, no. 3 (2011): 322–34.
20. Thomas Meehan, "What's Wrong with MARC?" SlideShare, last modified February 19, 2015, www.slideshare.net/orangeaurochs/whats-wrong-with-marc.
21. Ruben Verborgh and Seth van Hooland, *Linked Data for Libraries, Archives, and Museums: How to Clean, Link and Publish Your Metadata* (London: Facet, 2014).

3

MOTHERSHIP CONNECTIONS
URIs and Serializations

Chapter 2 introduced the Resource Description Framework (RDF), the foundational structure of the Semantic Web, and how RDF triples provide an alternative to representing knowledge through MARC. This leaves us with a framework and some rough ideas, but no concrete examples to speak of. It's time to get our hands dirty with the practical, everyday side of creating, identifying, and representing semantically rich linked data.

To do this, let's return to our hypothetical collection of funk and soul albums under consideration as a sample linked-data project. The first vinyl album we pulled out of the box was Parliament's *Mothership Connection*; we also retrieved a Library of Congress MARC record representing the same LP. If we take some of the information from the album sleeve and collate it with metadata from the MARC record, we can construct some useful statements about what we know of this particular item:

- It is an example of a musical album.
- It was released by Casablanca Records.

- It was issued in 1975.
- It was made by a musical group.
- The musical group that made it is called Parliament.
- Its catalog identifier is NBLP 7022.
- It has seven songs.
- It was produced by a person named George Clinton.
- The songs on the album were written, in aggregate, by George Clinton, Bootsy Collins, Bernie Worrell, Garry Shider, Glen Goins, and Jerome Brailey.
- Its genre is funk music.
- Its running time is 39 minutes.
- LC's control number for this album is 00717929.
- OCLC has a similar bibliographic record for this record, and its identifier is ocm03126136.

These characteristics are called *attributes*, which exist to describe nodes—again, some person, place, object, or concept in the real world—and their relationships with other nodes. Essentially, each node is made up of relationship connections; *Mothership Connection* is connected to its performer (Parliament), its record label (Casablanca Records), its producer (George Clinton), its genre (funk), the members of the band who performed on the album, and its seven individual songs.

As noted in chapter 2, RDF triples reduce everything in the world into either a thing or a thing's label. Data usually coalesces around the description of unique things, what we've been referring to as "nodes." In a table, for example, each row represents observations or attributes of a unique node; a MARC bibliographic record describes a node in the form of a single library resource, while authority records describe other nodes in the forms of people, groups of people, places, and concepts, to name just a few. As noted in chapter 2, literals describe identifying information not unlike the columns of a table, such as first and last names, birthdates, and Social Security numbers. (Note: Please *please* don't make a linked data record of yourself that contains your Social Security number.) Once we understand that difference, we can start broadly sorting our initial list of *Mothership Connection* details between the two structures, as seen in figure 3.1. (Once again, nodes are circular, literals are squares.)

Nodes appear in semantic data under two broad types: *classes* and *individuals*. If you are familiar with spreadsheets or databases, you will notice that each

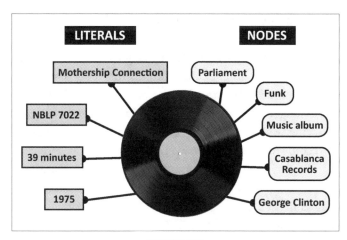

FIGURE 3.1
Nodes and literals

table row usually describes the characteristics of a single, one-of-a-kind thing: people (e.g., Michelle Obama), places (e.g., Portland), and things (e.g., the Taj Mahal). These are referred to as *individual nodes*, and they are also examples of *class nodes*. Classes are generalized nodes and are used to describe individual nodes; if someone were to ask you "What's a 'Portland'?" you would probably raise an eyebrow and reply, "It's a city." Such is the point of RDF classes. When we talk about *Mothership Connection*, we are referring to an individual thing, which is also an example of a class of nodes, such as *musical album*. (Classes will be discussed again in chapter 4.)

Literals can be text strings, dates, or numbers; each literal has an associated *datatype* to ensure that the literal value is absolutely clear. Computers rely on datatypes to identify how they are supposed to use the data. For example, *Mothership Connection* was released in 1975; a linked data triple referencing this fact might be recorded as the literal "1975-00-00" with a time-date datatype, explicitly identifying this string as a point in time. If a datatype isn't declared, RDF automatically assumes that literals are just text strings.[1] Not declaring the date-time datatype would be problematic, since "1975" is only inherently meaningful as a date to human beings (or, more specifically, to human beings who use the Gregorian calendar). To a machine, "1975" is simply four numbers strung together until we explicitly tell it otherwise.

While the literal datatype is meant primarily to foster computer processing, there is also a special kind of literal datatype intended for both human and machine understanding: *language-tagged strings*, which are used to denote the written or spoken language of the literal. *Mothership Connection* is, of course, the album's common identifier; it is also a string of text written in the English language, which we want to explicitly note in the RDF. Does this mean we would need to include exact translations of "Mothership Connection" for every other language? Not necessarily. Language-tagged strings are used to denote the varying ways that humans identify nodes using language; however, Casablanca Records released *Mothership Connection* in Brazil, Germany, France, Spain, the Philippines, and Japan, among other countries, under its English title.[2] Consequently, it would not be incorrect to create French, German, or Japanese-tagged literals using the English title, because the album is already known in those regions by its English title.

You may be wondering how it is possible to efficiently keep track of nodes when any node's basic name can exist in any one of hundreds of languages. The simple answer is, we don't track nodes by their labels. Even though a title like *Mothership Connection* seems to have the cultural cachet to be identifiable anywhere by title alone, the truth is that semantic data does not employ label values as identifiers. This is precisely because there can be *so many ways* to identify any given node. In a way, RDF mimics humankind's methods of understanding: the word *cloud* represents an abstract concept that, overall, is not unique to a single geographical or cultural area. But the meaning of *cloud* is dependent on knowing the English language. Similarly, if you don't speak Turkish, *bulut* means nothing to you; however, *bulut* and *cloud* represent the same abstract concept. Thus, in a semantic dataset, neither word would be useful as a unique identifier for the node representing clouds.

The problem is, linked data requires *some* kind of method to differentiate nodes from one another, inside and outside of datasets. Take the situation in chapter 1 with Charlie Chaplin (the filmmaker) and Charlie Chaplin (the ragga singer): in real life, it would be incredibly easy to tell these two people apart, and if somehow you didn't know either of them, there's usually a film nerd or a music snob just a couple of feet away to lecture upon their differences in enormous detail. Sadly, computers don't have other computers that can mansplain the nuances of reggae's subgenres, or argue that *Monsieur Verdoux* is Chaplin's most underrated film. The Semantic Web needs a method to uniquely identify the concepts and resources we intend to describe, and just like with RDF, a method does exist.

URIs

In chapter 1, we mentioned the Uniform Resource Locator (URL) as a key component in the invention of the World Wide Web. That chapter also noted that the World Wide Web largely exists as a web of linked documents. Not coincidentally, if you were to study the structure of a URL, you might see a lot of similarities with file locations in hard drives; URL syntax appropriates the typical file-path format used by most operating systems, where a slash (/) or backslash (\) character separates directories and file names. On a Windows PC, the file-path to a picture of a cat stored inside a folder might look like this:

C:\Users\some-persons-account\Pictures\Camera_Export\otto.jpg

Now compare this to the syntax of a website of cat pictures:

http://www.somecatpictures.fake/all-cats/torties/tallulah.png

In essence, executing a URL in a web browser is really just asking some far-away server to locate a file and send it back to you. It's not unlike sending a self-addressed, stamped envelope to your friend's home address and getting a bunch of printed-out tweets in the mail a week later.

As the core technologies of the World Wide Web evolved, the URL was supposed to be revised as part of a multipart architecture plan that brought together URLs and Uniform Resource Names (URNs), a new scheme of unique and persistent identifiers for web resources.[3] This arrangement, however, never materialized, and eventually both URNs and URLs were condensed into a single web standard, the Universal Resource Identifier (URI).[4] As a result, a URI can describe either a web resource's location, its name, or both.

Being locators as well as identifiers makes URIs integral to linked data and the Semantic Web. In a 2006 blog entry (the one that gave birth to the term *linked data*), Tim Berners-Lee posited four rules for creating semantic data, and—spoiler alert!—each of them refers specifically to URIs:

1. Use URIs as the names of things in your dataset.

> Every entity in a semantic database requires a unique identifier for every node in your database; what's more, that unique identifier must be exposed to the internet via HTTP. "If it doesn't use the universal URI," wrote Berners-Lee, "we don't call it Semantic Web." (Note that here, "names" refers specifically to the identifiers of nodes, rather than a title or a personal name.)

2. Make them URIs delivered over the web so that people can look up those names.

> In the context of linked data, URIs may locate things over the web, but they should be thought of primarily as names, not web addresses. Figure 3.2 shows what happens when a user accesses a URI that represents George Clinton. The semantic database recognizes the URI as the name of the entity; however, since URIs can also locate things, the database converts the URI to a URL, and uses it to locate the RDF data stored on the database.

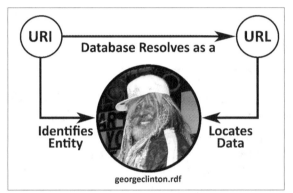

FIGURE 3.2
URI Diagram

3. When someone looks up your URIs, this should provide useful information using RDF.

> Accessing a URI should retrieve the triples of a particular node. Berners-Lee noted that in the first few years of the Semantic Web, research and evaluation projects produced significant amounts of data, but this data often existed as compressed or stored data, rather than being accessible on the web. Accessing a URI, he concluded, should lead to that node's machine-readable data—or even better, both human *and* machine-readable data.

4. Include links to other URIs, so that users can discover more things.

> Rule 4 is the cornerstone of linked data. Our Parliament node doesn't *have* to be connected to another node representing Parliament on another, music-focused semantic database, but honestly, why not link them? On the World Wide Web, "the value of your own information is very much a function of what it links to,

as well as the inherent value of the information within the web page," wrote Berners-Lee. "So it is also in the Semantic Web."[5]

DEEP DIVE
URIs vs. URLs: "I've Heard It Both Ways . . ."

At some point, you'll be discussing the finer points of linked data when someone will butt into your discussion, push his glasses up the bridge of his nose, and inform you that you're using the term URL when *actually* you mean URI. (Cue snide laughter.)

Ever since the release of the W3C's specifications for the URI syntax, IT nerds have engaged in the mindless pedantry of debating what constitutes a URI or a URL. See, the URI specification states: "A URI is a sequence of characters from a very limited set: the letters of the basic Latin alphabet, digits, and a few special characters. . . . The interpretation of a URI depends only on the characters used and not on how those characters are represented in a network protocol."[6] Translation: URIs don't always need to start with a network protocol (`http:`, `mailto:`, etc.), but URIs always do. This puts us in the odd position of having to state that *while almost all URLs are URIs, not all URIs are URLs.*

For some, this kind of technical sophistry is exactly why the internet was invented. But for a lot of other people, especially those with limited exposure to the intricacies of web technology (or those that just don't give a hoot), it's another avenue of—if you'll pardon the expression—the gatekeeping bullshit alluded to in the introduction of this book. The waters get even muddier with the latest W3C documents on RDF, which no longer mention URIs, but instead refer to *International Resource Identifiers* (IRIs), an expansion of URIs to allow the use of non-ASCII characters, such as Cyrillic and Asian language characters.[7]

So, when it comes to talking linked data, which is the right term to use? Well, the combination of a name and a network protocol is what turns a URI into a URL, and Berners-Lee's second rule of creating linked data explicitly instructs people to use HTTP URIs to make things findable. This means that, technically, HTTP URIs are . . . URLs.

In other words: *it doesn't matter.* Use whatever term you feel comfortable with, and use it with confidence. *Illegitimi non carborundum.*

DEEP DIVE
Things, Not Strings

A lot of the time, conversations explaining linked data usually present its reliance on URIs as identifiers without any in-depth discussion. Often, the explanation given is the slogan mentioned in chapter 2 ("Things, Not Strings"), which, as we noted, is actually a dodge from further explanation. Why should we follow the semantic model of using URIs to identify our data when our data already uses authority headings, ISBNs, and LC and OCLC control numbers?

Up to this point, we've talked about how computers don't understand human-created text, nor is human text immutably constructed or comprehended by humans. As useful as authority headings, ISBNs, and control numbers might be to us, they are still just strings of characters to computers. Imagine walking up to a complete stranger on the street, grabbing him by the shoulders, and asking, "I would like to know more about *Mothership Connection*, please!" Aside from scaring the wits out of this poor person, what are the chances that he actually knows the ins and outs of a popular funk album from the 1970s? As this person tries to get away, you say: "*Mothership Connection*! Casablanca Records catalog number NBLP 7022! LC control number 00717929!" Will reciting these attributes help you get the information you want if the person you've assaulted has no frame of reference for *Mothership Connection*? Our point here is that using text-string identifiers is no guarantee for finding bibliographic data inside an OPAC or an ILS.

Compare this with having a URI as the "name" of a thing. Each URI needs to point to an unambiguous, individual thing. There may be several URIs out there that each represent the same thing; linked data allows us to explicitly note this situation. When we are able to uniquely identify our collective knowledge and pool it all, we will be able to grab any and all information *about* these things without relying absolutely on searching strings of text for names or control numbers. And because the data connected to these URIs is highly atomized, we can give detailed instructions to a computer on how to process the data and send back reliable, consistent results every time.

To do this, however, our URIs, in addition to being unique, need to never change. The same cannot be said for ISBNs and control numbers. ISBNs are not supposed to be reused, but mix-ups and typos happen all the time; similarly, a control number is never a guarantee for a permanent identifier, as records can always be merged. And then there's authority records, which change *constantly*. Humans are always reevaluating and revising the ways in which we describe things; as of this writing, there is a small but concerted effort to revise library authorities to remove a pervasive bias of the point-of-view of white people and men. As these descriptions change, their control numbers stay the same, but the headings themselves—strings of text residing in thousands or millions of records of MARC records—need to be changed manually.

For a second, imagine a system where authority headings are not recorded in library data as strings of text but as URIs; when a record is pulled up, the system queries the URI, finds data, and returns it to the cataloger (or patron) looking at the record. It no longer matters if the heading has changed, because the text of the heading is simply a literal value returned from the RDF data residing underneath the URI. This is what is meant by "Things, Not Strings": a shift away from text-based identifiers to *things*, represented by URIs and containing RDF underneath.

Now that we're ready to start looking at codifying triples, we can revisit some of the characteristics and details we collected about *Mothership Connection* from its sleeve notes and the Library of Congress MARC record. The process of creating and publishing URIs for data is referred to as *minting* URIs. Since our example case is purely hypothetical, we will use fake URIs to stand in for where an institution would mint actual URIs connected to semantic data. Figure 3.3 shows a handful of our fake URIs representing previously identified nodes, as well as an external link to the *Mothership Connection* entity in TuneEggheadz, a (nonexistent) database about music:

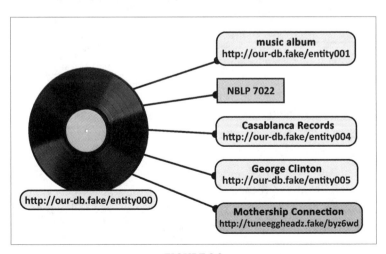

FIGURE 3.3
Mothership Connection as RDF, take 1

These statements can also be represented using a table:

SUBJECT	PREDICATE	OBJECT
Mothership Connection	is a kind of	Music album
Mothership Connection	has the catalog number	NBLP 7022
Mothership Connection	was released by	Casablanca Records
Mothership Connection	was produced by	George Clinton
Mothership Connection	was performed by	Parliament
Mothership Connection	is the same as another node located at	[TuneEggheadz URI]

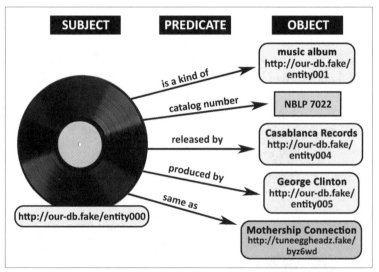

FIGURE 3.4
Mothership Connection as RDF, take 2

Figure 3.4 employs orientation arrows to show the relational direction of each statement; in this diagram, *Mothership Connection* is the subject connected to other objects. However, these arrows also imply that reciprocal statements are now possible in some cases; based on figure 3.3, the following triples are implied to be true, and thus could also be added:

SUBJECT	PREDICATE	OBJECT
George Clinton	Produced	*Mothership Connection*
Parliament	Performed	*Mothership Connection*
Casablanca Records	Released	*Mothership Connection*
[TuneEggheadz URI]	is the same as another node located at	*Mothership Connection*

However, before we charge off creating new reciprocal relationships for other entities, clever readers may have already picked up on the fact that our existing predicate statements are text statements, and thus not machine-readable. If you have followed along this far, it probably won't surprise you that the predicates between entities and literal values—referred to in RDF as *properties*—also require unique URIs. Just as a node is a series of triples identified by a URI, a property is a series of triples intended to help machines understand connections to other entities and literals. Once again, we use fake URIs as a stand-in for properties we would normally create (and mint with URIs) later on, leaving us with the final linked-data diagram pictured in figure 3.5.

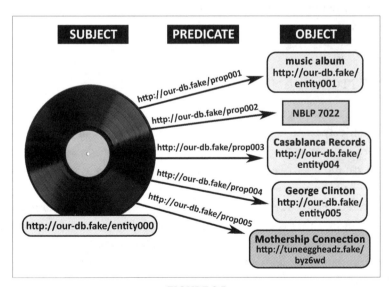

FIGURE 3.5
Mothership Connection as RDF, take 3

We can now swap out all of our textual representations of the relationships and entities:

SUBJECT	PREDICATE	OBJECT
http://our-db.fake/entity000	http://ourdb.org/prop001	http://our-db.fake/entity001
http://our-db.fake/entity000	http://ourdb.org/prop002	NBLP 7022
http://our-db.fake/entity000	http://ourdb.org/prop003	http://our-db.fake/entity004
http://our-db.fake/entity000	http://ourdb.org/prop004	http://our-db.fake/entity005
http://our-db.fake/entity000	http://ourdb.org/prop005	http://our-db.fake/entity006
http://our-db.fake/entity000	http://ourdb.org/prop006	http://tuneeggheadz.fake/byz6wd

Believe it or not, this table is effectively a faithful, near-complete example of linked data. Our URIs do not actually identify or locate semantic resources, but these triple statements are the essence of linked data. Of course, modeling data as arrows and squircles is a helpful way to conceptualize and visualize relationships, but they ultimately are not machine-readable. In order for us to turn our models into something accessible, we will need to (a) translate our triples into a syntax that machines will understand, and (b) figure out where to put those translations.

TRIPLESTORES AND SERIALIZATIONS

Recall that a collection of RDF triples can be stored in a kind of graph database, unimaginatively termed a *triplestore*. How is the data stored and structured in triplestores? This question is hard to answer. Some triplestores are scratch-built from the ground up, while some exist as layers built on top of an already existing database. Apache Jena and AllegroGraph are examples of open-source and commercial triplestore systems, respectively, that were built with unique graph database engines that eschew the mechanisms of typical relational database management systems. On the opposite side is OpenLink Virtuoso, where data can be represented through either traditional relational tables or RDF graphs.

Beyond these storage differences, many triplestore systems share a basic function: SPARQL access. SPARQL (SPARQL Protocol and RDF Query Language) is a query language and a protocol for traversing RDF data. (And yes, it's pronounced *sparkle*.) If you've ever worked with SQL (Structured Query

Language), you might see similarities between the two languages. SQL is used to query relational databases by finding related information from disparate tables, stitching the data together, and returning it as a new, highly detailed table. SPARQL, on the other hand, can be used to execute similarly complex RDF queries over multiple graphs, validate the structure of a graph, and even add new triples to existing RDF data. SPARQL queries are often used for synthesizing specific knowledge from RDF, but they can also be valuable for scripting purposes; web crawlers, for example, can be deployed to automatically harvest Semantic Web content using SPARQL queries. (See chapter 5 for a real-world SPARQL example.)

Triplestores and SPARQL searches sound cool, but so far, we have only a handful of triples to show for our work. As of right now, it doesn't make sense for us to go through the work of acquiring a server, setting up a triplestore, and deploying our linked data to the world. Smaller datasets containing a small number of triples are better served as an RDF file stored locally—or better yet, published to the web using a known RDF *serialization*. Serialization is when data is converted to a different format without losing the original, underlying structure. The next section briefly explains several kinds of RDF serializations that are currently available.

RDF/XML

In the late 1990s, as the Semantic Web was growing from a theoretical concept into a full-fledged data model, the first W3C implementation of the Extensible Markup Language (XML) was released. XML enjoyed a fairly immediate popularity due to its support of a wide variety of applications, and it remains a WC3-recommended data format. When the first RDF data model was published in 1999, it was defined alongside an XML serialization, *RDF/XML*. This was considered a sensible decision, considering how popular XML was at the time.[8] Unfortunately, it had the unintended effect of leading people to assume that RDF *was* XML, requiring Berners-Lee to explicitly delineate the two soon after.[9] (Apparently, this still needs to be reiterated twenty years on.)[10] On the practical side, people soon realized that RDF/XML, as a format for delivering RDF data, was verbose, tedious to create by hand, difficult to parse without special tools, and just plain butt-ugly to the eye, even though one of the format's goals was to produce machine-readable data that was also "human-legible and reasonably clear."[11] Not too long afterward, other RDF serializations were introduced, and the omnipresence of RDF/XML faded, although it never completely went away. The likelihood of your needing to know RDF/XML now or in the future is pretty low; accordingly, we won't be showing it off here.

N-TRIPLES

Not surprisingly, the succeeding RDF serialization formats went in a completely opposite direction from RDF/XML. *N-Triples*, for example, is an RDF format that focuses on serving complete triple statements on single lines.[12] Each line of N-Triple data represents a single triple, with its subject, predicate, and object separated by single spaces; the triples are written in plain-text format, meaning they require no special text formatting to indicate them as RDF statements. Taking the idea of a triple-as-a-sentence to its logical conclusion, each N-Triple statement ends with a period; a new line signifies the next triple. Our sample data converted to N-Triples looks like this:

```
00 <http://our-db.fake/entity000> <http://our-db.fake/
prop001> <http://our-db.fake/entity001> .

01 <http://our-db.fake/entity000> <http://our-db.fake/
prop002> "NBLP 7022" .

02 <http://our-db.fake/entity000> <http://our-db.fake/
prop003> <http://our-db.fake/entity004> .

03 <http://our-db.fake/entity000> <http://our-db.fake/
prop004> <http://our-db.fake/entity005> .

04 <http://our-db.fake/entity000> <http://our-db.fake/
prop005> <http://our-db.fake/entity006> .

05 <http://our-db.fake/entity000> <http://our-db.fake/
prop006> <http://tuneeggheadz.fake/byz6wd> .
```

Note that angle brackets indicate the presence of a URI and quotation marks notate literal values. Literal datatypes can be referenced, depending on the literal; if we wanted to add the release date of *Mothership Connection* using a new property (http://our-db.fake/prop007), we could add another URI that denotes date-formatted text used in XML schemas:

```
06 <http://our-db.fake/entity000> <http://our-db.
fake/prop007> "1975-00-00"^^<http://www.w3.org/2001/
XMLSchema#date> .
```

Here, the URI (http://www.w3.org/2001/XMLSchema#date) alerts a computer that this particular literal should be processed as a date object, not just as a string of text.

The N-Triples format, much like XML, can be cumbersome when hand-coding large amounts of data. Furthermore, N-Triples leave us with interminably long lines, as we redundantly reuse URIs. Fortunately, there is yet another, related serialization that further simplifies RDF for human consumption.

TURTLE

Turtle—short for "Terse RDF Triple Language"—represents something of a compromise between N-Triples and RDF/XML. Rather than repeat a triple's subject on every single line, Turtle allows for a compact version of N-Triple data, grouping objects and predicates that share a single node. Below is perfectly legal Turtle for our sample data:

```
<http://our-db.fake/entity000>
    <http://our-db.fake/prop001> <http://our-db.fake/
    entity001> ;
    <http://our-db.fake/prop002> "NBLP 7022" ;
    <http://our-db.fake/prop003> <http://our-db.fake/
    entity004> ;
    <http://our-db.fake/prop004> <http://our-db.fake/
    entity005> ;
    <http://our-db.fake/prop005> <http://our-db.fake/
    entity006> ;
    <http://our-db.fake/prop006> <http://tuneeggheadz.fake/
    byz6wd> .
```

Instead of a series of statements, Turtle can create a run-on sentence featuring a single subject. Each object-predicate pair is separated by a semicolon, the last one closing with a period; finally, predicate-object pairs can be indented for the sake of readability. Not too shabby!

But Turtle can do even more for RDF data. Including full URIs for both objects and predicates still takes up quite a bit of code space; this can be curtailed using *namespace declarations*:

```
@prefix odb: <http://our-db.fake/> .
@prefix eggheadz: <http://tuneeggheadz.fake/> .

odb:entity000
    odb:prop001 odb:entity001 ;
    odb:prop002 "NBLP 7022" ;
    odb:prop003 odb:entity004 ;
    odb:prop004 odb:entity005 ;
    odb:prop005 odb:entity006 ;
    odb:prop006 eggheadz:byz6wd .
```

The idea is that there's no need to repeatedly use a long URI prefix; instead, we declare what's known in computer programming as "variables" that stand in the part of the URI that doesn't change. Then, in the body of the Turtle, we swap out those URI prefixes for our variables. The overall effect not only declutters the visual space of the code, but is also somewhat easier for the human eye to parse.

JSON-LD

Our last RDF serialization is also the newest of the bunch: *JSON-LD*. Originally based on a subset of the JavaScript programming language, JavaScript Object Notation (JSON) became a language-independent data serialization and messaging format. JSON was originally touted as an alternative to XML, promising "the same benefits of interoperability and openness," but without being "ugly and inefficient."[13] Whether you agree or not, at this point, JSON is the primary data-interchange game in town; if you've ever used the internet, some information has been delivered to you as JSON data, whether you know it or not.

Much like XML, JSON is a customizable data format, but it prioritizes syntax over schemas. That syntax prioritizes aggregate types of data structures—attribute-value pairs (similar to the key-value system found in databases) and

```
{
        "albums": [ {
                "title": "Mothership Connection",
                "artist": {
                        "name": "Parliament",
                        "founded": 1974,
                        "ended": 1980
                },
                "year": 1975,
                "label": "Casablanca Records",
                "catalog": "NBLP 7022",
                "producer": "George Clinton",
                "genre": "funk"
        }
    ]
}
```

arrays (or lists of data)—along with strings, numbers, and boolean (`true` and `false`) values. Our sample data could be converted to JSON as follows:

In this sample JSON data, our root node indicates a collection of data representing a list of albums (although we only have a single album record). As in the syntax of XML, we can nest attribute-value pairs and lists within each other; using nested data, we can create richer JSON data, such as our "`artist`" attribute containing data describing Parliament as an album's artist.

Considering JSON's popularity and ubiquity in the delivery of web content and data, it seemed only natural to merge it with the Semantic Web. `JSON-LD`—or JSON Linked Data—is an RDF serialization that uses JSON

objects to express RDF triples. Once again, we run our sample triples through
the format and come away with the serialization below:

```
{
        "@context": {
                "odb": {
                        "@id": "http://ourdb.org/","@prefix": true
                },
                "eggheadz": {
                        "@id": "http://tuneeggheadz.fake/",
                        "@prefix": true
                },
                "odb:prop003": {
                        "@type": "@id"
                },
                "odb:prop004": {
                        "@type": "@id"
                },
                "odb:prop005": {
                        "@type": "@id"
                },
                "odb:prop006": {
                        "@type": "@id"
                }
        },
        "@id": "odb:entity000",
        "@type": "odb:entity001",
        "odb:prop002": "NBLP 7022",
        "odb:prop003": "odb:entity004",
        "odb:prop004": "odb:entity005",
        "odb:prop005": "odb:entity006",
        "odb:prop006": "eggheadz:byz6wd"
}
```

The similarities to Turtle are noticeable; our JSON-LD object begins with a `@context` data object, where we set our namespace shortcuts, odb and egg-headz. Below that, we use JSON-LD's built-in `@type` attribute to describe our node, rather than the type property (prop001) we set up to identify Mothership Connection as a musical album. We also identify the URI for our Mothership Connection object (entity000) with an `@id` attribute; this is called the node identifier in JSON-LD. We're using it in two ways here; by itself, `@id` represents the URI for the subject of the JSON-LD block (i.e., Mothership Connection). However, we know ahead of time that some of our predicate values—released by (prop003), produced by (prop004), and same as (prop005)—will have object values that are going to be URIs, not text or numbers. So, we have to spend some space of the `@context` area explicitly identifying ahead of time that we expect those values are going to be URIs.

If it seems a bit weird to be front-loading so much work in identifying RDF subjects as URIs when triple subjects are almost always URIs . . . well, it's not just you. The short, diplomatic answer is that in the process of hammering the JSON format to fit within the general RDF model, a number of compromises were made, based on the structure of the JSON format. As a data syntax, JSON was built to transfer strings of text, numbers, and booleans between servers and computers; consequently, the JSON-LD model is better suited to handle triple objects mostly made of literals, like *Mothership Connection*'s title, rather than URI objects. Knowing this, it probably won't surprise you to learn that Manu Sporny, one of the primary creators of JSON-LD and the lead editor of the W3C's first JSON-LD specification, has little love for RDF as a data model. "I hate the narrative of the Semantic Web because the focus has been on the wrong set of things for a long time," Sporny wrote in 2014. "Precious time is spent in groups discussing how we can query all this Big Data that is sure to be published via RDF instead of figuring out a way of making it easy to publish that data on the Web by leveraging common practices in use today. . . . I like JSON-LD because it's based on technology that most web developers use today. . . . It helps you get to the 'adjacent possible,' instead of having to wait for a mirage to solidify."[14]

RETURNING TO THE MOTHERSHIP

At this point, you have created a number of nodes and properties around a single album from the special collection. Satisfied with the results so far, you move on to the next album in the collection: *One Nation Under a Groove*. Much like the other LP, the record sleeve has generous amounts of information like songwriting credits, year, label, and an overall funky disposition. You start collating the information, just as you did before:

- It was released by Warner Bros. Records in 1978.
- It was performed by a musical group called Funkadelic.
- Its catalog identifier is WB 56-539.
- It has six tracks on a 12-inch LP, with a further three songs on an accompanying bonus seven-inch record.
- Again, the genre is funk music.
- Its running time is 58 minutes.
- It was produced by George Clinton.
- The songs on the album were written, in aggregate, by George Clinton, Walter Morrison, Garry Shider, Bernie Worrell, Michael Hampton, Linda Brown, Bootsy Collins, and Edward Hazel.

Some of those names will seem familiar to you. After doing a quick internet check, it turns out that Funkadelic is, in fact, inextricably linked to Parliament. From what you read online, Parliament began as a doo-wop act that soon morphed into a funk and soul group. A legal dispute with their record label meant that the band temporarily lost the rights to their name; George Clinton rebranded the group Funkadelic, changed their style to a more psychedelic flavor of funk, and signed them to a different label. Later, in the early 1970s, Clinton regained the rights to the name Parliament. Clinton subsequently signed the members of Funkadelic to a different record label, this time under the Parliament moniker. As a result, Clinton was the bandleader of two different outfits made up of the same musicians: Funkadelic played psychedelic funk and rock, while Parliament released good-time dance and funk music. The whole bunch would tour billed as Parliament-Funkadelic, or more simply, P-Funk. "P-Funk" would later come to describe the collective of over fifty musicians in and around the two bands, including offshoot groups founded by P-Funk collaborators, like Bootsy Collins's Rubber Band and the P-Funk All Stars; P-Funk also came to describe the style of music promulgated by the bands, as well as their aesthetic and mythology.

Up until this point, we have created both nodes and properties as we saw fit in order to describe what lay before us. Our handful of properties will suffice in describing *One Nation Under a Groove*, but what about the relationship between Parliament and Funkadelic? How does one describe a complicated tie-in formed of both legal and aesthetic choices? Are they two separate bands that happen to share similar membership? Do they have an explicit connection between the two of them, and if so, how is that connection defined? Or are they separate manifestations of a larger collective of musicians? And if so, how does the term P-Funk, with its use in describing both a mythology and a musical-performance style, fit in?

All of these questions are but to remind ourselves that any attempt to categorize and classify waking life will be complicated and frustrating, as life can be. The next chapter addresses some of these concerns as we investigate ontologies, which define the nodes, properties, and relations found in a linked dataset.

NOTES

1. Jose Emilio labra Gayo, Eric Prud'hommeaux, Iovka Boneva, and Dimitris Kontokostas, *Validating RDF Data*, Synthesis Lectures on the Semantic Web: Theory and Technology 7, no. 1 (2018), http://book.validatingrdf.com/bookHtml008.html.

2. Discogs, "Parliament—Mothership Connection," www.discogs.com/Parliament-Mother ship-Connection/master/15841.

3. K. Sollins and L. Masinter, "Functional Requirements for Uniform Resource Names," Network Working Group, IETF Tools, last modified December 1994, https://tools.ietf .org/html/rfc1737.

4. World Wide Web Consortium, W3C/IETF URI Planning Interest Group, "URIs, URLs, and URNs: Clarifications and Recommendations 1.0," last modified September 21, 2001, www.w3.org/TR/uri-clarification/.

5. Tim Berners-Lee, "Linked Data: Design Issues," World Wide Web Consortium, last modified June 18, 2009, www.w3.org/DesignIssues/LinkedData.html.

6. Tim Berners-Lee, R. Fielding, and L. Masinter, "Uniform Resource Identifier (URI): Generic Syntax," Network Working Group, IETF Tools, last modified January 2005, https://tools.ietf.org/html/rfc3986.

7. World Wide Web Consortium, "RDF 1.1 Primer," last modified June 24, 2014, www .w3.org/TR/rdf11-primer/.

8. Gayo et al., *Validating RDF Data*, http://book.validatingrdf.com/bookHtml007.html.

9. Tim Berners-Lee, "Semantic Web: Why RDF Is More Than XML," World Wide Web Consortium, last modified October 14, 1998, www.w3.org/DesignIssues/RDF-XML .html.

10. Mark Schubert, "RDF Is Not XML: RDF Serialization and iiRDS Metadata," Parson, last modified December 4, 2018, www.parson-europe.com/de/wissensartikel/557-rdf-is -not-xml-rdf-serialization-and-iirds-metadata.html.

11. World Wide Web Consortium, "Extensible Markup Language (XML) 1.0 (Fifth Edition)," last modified February 7, 2013, www.w3.org/TR/REC-xml/.

12. World Wide Web Consortium, "RDF 1.1 N-Triples: A Line-Based Syntax for an RDF Graph," last modified February 25, 2014, www.w3.org/TR/n-triples/.

13. JSON.org, "JSON: The Fat-Free Alternative to XML," www.json.org/xml.html.

14. Manu Sporny, "JSON-LD and Why I Hate the Semantic Web," Manu.Sporny.org, last modified January 21, 2014, archived from the original at https://web.archive.org/web/20190405035404/; http://manu.sporny.org/2014/json-ld-origins-2/.

WHAT IS A THING?
Ontologies and Linked Data

One is what one is, partly at least.
—Samuel Beckett, *Molloy*

I t's time for us to dig a bit deeper.

Librarians organize and provide information, and when you think about it, that's a pretty big responsibility. But defining what something *is* so it can be found later . . . that's an act of truth-telling. What are the truths that are accepted and shared so solidly that we can encode them into our systems? We make these kinds of calls every day so that information can be sorted and furnished upon request; but thinking about how these decisions sculpt our reality, how they define what is and what can be inferred—well, that's *heady stuff.* But we need to reflect on it for a moment, because our work in representing information is pretty powerful. Consequently, this chapter dips into the philosophical realm, with a short trip to the land of computer science before moving on to library and information science, all in the service of exploring the term *ontology* and how it matters specifically to linked data.

In the world of philosophy, ontology is the study of being, and is concerned with existence and the nature of reality. (Like we said, *heady stuff.*) Put more simply, ontology questions what things exist in life, and how those things can be categorized based on their similarities and differences. Through this kind of investigation, ontology is ultimately how we humans decide how we refer (or don't refer) to the things around us. *Ontology* has a somewhat different but related meaning in the worlds of computer science and the Semantic Web. In these worlds, an *ontology* is an abstract model representing some domain of knowledge. An ontology rarely changes and is designed to enable knowledge accumulation and its sharing, reuse, or processing.[1] So, if the Semantic Web is human knowledge codified as machine-understandable data, then when we refer to a particular *linked data ontology*, we're talking about the set of rules for organizing and defining a specific subset of human knowledge as that kind of data.

Ontologies suffer from a bit of an identity crisis, which can be confusing when people try to explain them, or their concrete relationship to linked data, in detail. One reason for this is that ontology design has grown out of several distinct disciplines; depending on your background, certain aspects of ontologies may be emphasized or downplayed. But rest assured that, as a librarian, you are already way ahead of the game in understanding the basic concepts of ontologies. Let's get oriented with a look at how ontologies are defined for linked data purposes, and then we'll talk a bit more about just how uniquely poised library and information professionals are in contributing to the linked data cloud.

DEFINITIONS

The most commonly referenced definition of *ontology* nowadays comes out of computer science, and it's only slightly less vague than the one that came from philosophy class. Stanford University's Thomas Gruber defined ontologies as an "explicit specification of a conceptualization."[2] This was further refined by Willem Nico Borst as a "formal specification of a shared conceptualization."[3] These two definitions are important because they underline that ontologies are specifications (rules) that deal with concepts (information) in a formal (standard) and shared (community-accepted) way. Does this sound familiar? It should—librarians have been doing this for basically *forever*.

What these definitions do not explicitly reveal is that the community of computer science got interested in ontologies because they turned out to be a huge asset for computers to quickly index and retrieve information. According to the information professionals Joseph Tennis and Javier Calzada-Prado, computer scientists began pushing for ontologies, but what they were really asking for was "semantically richer vocabularies" that could be used by artificial intelligence to make reasonable assumptions about sets of data.[4] Indeed, ontologies are key to a plethora of data-driven projects; artificial intelligence (AI) researchers, for example, use ontology concepts to train computers to create frameworks that make sense of large amounts of data, or to predict behavior based on that data. While working on large bodies of text, computers routinely perform natural language processing, clustering, text analysis, and other machine learning techniques to create these frameworks.

Librarians aren't blazing the trail on AI, but that does not mean that the components of ontology development are completely alien to the library community. In fact, librarians already work with quite a few of the building blocks of basic ontologies; a definition by David Stuart of King's College London suggests that *ontology*, as a term, exists on a spectrum, its meaning dependent on how it is used. For Stuart, an ontology can either be "a catch-all term for the various types of formalized vocabularies that exist to express concepts and the relationships among them"—namely, controlled vocabularies, taxonomies, and metadata schemas—or a more restrictive usage that focuses on a particular data model (like the set of relationships that we created to describe *Mothership Connection* in chapter 2).[5] Many cataloging and technical librarians work with controlled vocabularies every day in disambiguating similar names and subject terms. As we saw in chapter 2, it is also common for thesauri to decide if broader or narrower terms are appropriate to describe some thing's *aboutness*. These two concepts—defining the language used ("What does 'music album' mean?") and assigning relationships to the terms in the vocabulary—are absolutely central to ontology development.

The W3C, interestingly, seems to conflate the terms *ontology* and *vocabulary* as they pertain to the Semantic Web. The W3C defines vocabularies in much the same way that we have already described ontologies, noting that vocabularies "are used to classify the terms that can be used in a particular application, characterize possible relationships, and define possible constraints on using those terms."[6] A number of librarians would probably disagree with such an amalgamation of terms; as depicted in chapter 2, some of the Library of Congress's name and subject vocabularies include relationships between other terms in the thesaurus, but the choices made in selecting name and subject headings also reflect decisions regarding regional and dialectal spellings, the intended audience, and condensing synonyms into a single heading. In comparison, what seems to make ontologies more "formal"—that is, richer—than a vocabulary is the scope and level of detail in their relationships. For instance, our data model from chapter 3 includes a number of thoughtful ways to describe a single music album, along with its relationships with its creators, its record label, and its genre. But in diving in without a larger game plan (ontology), we're left with a model which only partially describes that album, and certainly not one adapted to fit *any* album. What's more, our model has not accounted for more than a few related nodes; to be of use in a linked data environment, our model needs to be able to let a computer infer information at both a specific, granular degree (i.e., What is *Mothership Connection?*) and all the way to the universal, upper levels of description. (How do we define music? Albums? Bands? Human beings?) In other words, an ontology is designed with a specific set of questions that it should be able to answer. Ontologies with expressive, articulate representations of knowledge take more time to build and more time to apply, but effectively deliver more accurate representations of knowledge in linked data systems.

TYPES OF ONTOLOGIES

Depending on the objective, different sorts of ontologies may need to be explored to select an appropriate tool for the purpose. Recall that ontology definitions are somewhat fluid, and that the term *ontology* often denotes a spectrum of tools that vary in depth and/or richness. The following types of ontologies—built upon definitions created by Dieter Fensel, director of the Semantic Technologies Institute Innsbruck at the University of Innsbruck, Austria—are listed from the most specific to the broadest in character.[7]

Domain ontologies and vocabularies (or *domain-specific ontologies*) are grounded in a specific community, topic, or discipline and are designed to represent the concepts most integral to that area. A domain ontology might focus on music, medicine, or geography and contains terms defined according to that domain's interpretations. Terms are differentiated from how they are applied within other disciplines and represent the shared understanding of the domain's subject expertise. Different ontologies within the same domain may arise and at times be in conflict or need to be mapped, or merged. Examples include the Music Ontology (http://musicontology.com/), a vocabulary for linking a wide range of music-related data; and the Disease Ontology (http://disease-ontology.org/), which provides the biomedical community with descriptions of human disease terms and related medical concepts.

Likewise, there are also many *metadata schema ontologies* in use that are foundational to developing models for different sets of data. By working with these standards and modeling data in shared ways, these metadata schemas support the transition to Semantic Web models. Many of these schemas have active communities researching, debating, and publishing decisions that support the use of structured data ontologies. Metadata schema ontologies may be either domain-specific or general, and usually have roots in a metadata standard used in application profiles and metadata creation. Examples include the Dublin Core Metadata Initiative (http://dublincore.org/about/), a general metadata schema that is widely used in digital library repositories; and the Visual Resources Association (VRA) Core (http://vraweb.org/vra-core-rdf -ontology-available-for-review/), the Library of Congress descriptive standard for art and visual works.

Moving just slightly beyond the scope of this chapter are *aggregate data models*. Like metadata ontologies, they provide a framework for a large community; however, instead of providing a schema that community members are expected to use, these data models offer a method in which data contributors supply their own diverse and disparate metadata, which is then mapped to the data, which is a single, interoperable data structure. An example is the Europeana Data Model (EDM), which bills itself as "an anchor to which various finer-grained models can be attached, making them at least partly interoperable at the semantic level."[8]

Finally, *upper*, *core*, or *generic ontologies* consist of very general terms that are not domain-specific but rather serve wider purposes, such as serving as the "glue" needed to semantically describe basic, largely universal relationships, or to bring together other domain ontologies for interoperability. In fact, RDF is associated with several core, generic ontologies, the two most common being the RDF Syntax (known with the prefix `rdf`) and RDF Schema (known as `rdfs`).[9] The `rdf` ontology focuses on the basic description of resources (individual nodes), while `rdfs` helps define and describe classes. Together, these two provide "resources that can be used to describe other RDF resources in application-specific RDF vocabularies"—which is to say, basic elements for creating ontologies and identifying things as resources.[10]

Though these two core ontologies provide the rock-bottom basics for creating ontologies, it soon became clear that more expressive languages were needed to put the Semantic Web to effective use. The result was a group of more formal descriptive languages for creating ontologies, collectively referred to as the Web Ontology Language (OWL). The particulars of the OWL language family could fill a book by themselves, but suffice it to say that OWL has enriched our ability to express knowledge and relationships semantically, in both nodes and properties.

Together, rdf, rdfs, and OWL are the foundation of most, if not all, linked data ontologies, including one of the oldest. Friend-of-a-Friend (FOAF) was designed to describe people, their relation to other people, their activities, and objects. (Despite much excitement—Berners-Lee once wrote: "I express my network in a FOAF file, and that is a start of the revolution"—the adoption of FOAF has been quite low.)[11] RDF is also the basis for SKOS (Simple Knowledge Organization System), a W3C ontology originally designed by the library and archives software developer Ed Summers for representing thesauri, taxonomies, classification schemes, and subject heading lists as semantic data. SKOS was designed to provide a simplified, lightweight solution to migrate existing organization systems to the Semantic Web. The Library of Congress's subjects, thesauri, classification scheme, names, and cataloging and preservation vocabularies are largely available in SKOS-formatted linked data at LC's Linked Data Service at http://id.loc.gov, which we will cover in a later chapter.

CLASSES AND PROPERTIES

To build our worlds, we need to understand some of the pieces of a linked data ontology. The W3C defines an ontology with a handful of major components—namely, classes and properties.[12] *Classes*, which we touched on in chapter 3, are nodes grouped together by shared, general qualities. (Examples of classes in our hypothetical linked dataset are *Humans*, *Bands*, and *Music Albums*.) This is where the domain or scope of the dataset becomes vitally important: if you recognize that many of your entities share the same kind of embodied qualities, then it's probably a good idea to create a class entity as a specific category. Moving in the opposite direction, *individuals* are one-of-a-kind examples of nodes that belong to one (or more) classes. Individuals are generally proper nouns, such as Michelle Obama, Portland, or the Taj Mahal. *Mothership Connection* is an individual of our invented class, *Music Album*.

When every individual in a class does not share the same qualities as all other individuals, it may be necessary to create *subclasses* to differentiate entity types. For example, Parliament-Funkadelic could be an example of the class *Band*, a group of people who perform music together. However, that definition could also apply to a sixty-piece classical orchestra, which, according to our cultural conventions, is quite different from a band. The smarter approach might be to make both *Band* and *Orchestra* subclass entities of a third, *Music Ensemble*, which could contain further subclasses, such as *Vocal Group*, *Musical Duo*, and so on.[13] Finally, *properties* represent the relationships in ontologies. If this sounds familiar, it's because we mentioned properties in the context of triple predicates in chapter 3. Properties can have restrictions on how they are used, such as whether a property is required for a certain class of entity.[14]

Sewn together, these elements help answer some important questions about the knowledge we are trying to represent, including:

1. What are our classes, and what properties do we need to show relationships?

   Since our makeshift data model is intended to describe a collection of funk and soul albums, it would make sense for us to define a class called *Music Album*. At the same time, we have already implicitly created the need to define classes for bands, humans, companies, and music genres, as well as the need for properties showing production credits, songwriting, instrumentation, release dates, and so on. What is the expected scope of our data, and how far-reaching does it need to be to accurately describe the collection?

2. Will there be subclasses, and if so, are they hierarchical?

   Wikidata is a popular linked dataset that underpins the data found in many Wikimedia projects, such as *Wikipedia*. (Wikidata is discussed in detail in chapter 5.) Figure 4.1 shows a very small subset of hierarchical classes found in the ontology of Wikidata, starting with *album* and ending at *creative work*. This may seem like overkill, but Wikidata's lofty ambition is to produce a dataset where just about anything, living or dead, can be described. (Note that *creative work* isn't even the top of the hierarchy for *album*—it extends all the way up to *entity*, Wikidata's uppermost class, making it the most basic description of anything in the world!) This means their ontology has the flexibility to express richer knowledge than our single-level *music album* class. On the other hand, if all we have on hand is a couple boxes that really are just albums, then maybe the hierarchy of our makeshift project needn't be so intense. Again, it all depends on defining our scope.

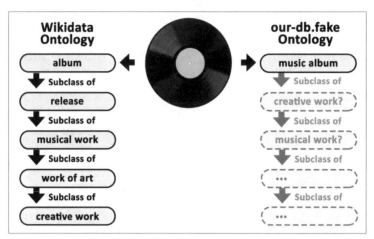

FIGURE 4.1
Comparison of Wikidata's ontology and our (fake) ontology

3. What things within our data are equivalent?

Herein lies the Parliament-Funkadelic relationship question posed at the end of chapter 3. Are they simply two individuals belonging to the same class? Or is there a property that can be used to show a unique relationship between them?

4. Which things require inverse relationships and which do not?

George Clinton, the leader of Parliament-Funkadelic and producer of *Mothership Connection*, is an individual of a class representing people (for example, *human*). An inverse of that triple—one which states that the *human* class is exemplified through an individual entity like George Clinton—is unnecessary. Not only would this become cumbersome if the dataset needs to scale upward, but most semantic databases already employ SPARQL, which allows users to search an entire linked database for specific information. A SPARQL query could easily be written to find all entities described with the class *human* in a semantic dataset. (SPARQL will be discussed in chapter 5.) Yet there are circumstances when an equal and inverse triple is warranted, and even necessary.

CASE IN POINT
Produced By vs. Producer Of

Our example from chapters 2 and 3 includes the following triples:

SUBJECT	PREDICATE	OBJECT
Mothership Connection	produced by	George Clinton
Mothership Connection	performed by	Parliament
Mothership Connection	released by	Casablanca Records

In chapter 3, we noted that these triples imply that two inverse statements should also be true:

SUBJECT	PREDICATE	OBJECT
George Clinton	Produced	*Mothership Connection*
Parliament	Performed	*Mothership Connection*
Casablanca Records	Released	*Mothership Connection*

Together, these create two-way relationships between *Mothership Connection* and the two entities. However, unless we explicitly add those triples to the entity records of George Clinton and Casablanca Records, this information will only exist within the entity for *Mothership Connection*. So if we were to construct a SPARQL query to retrieve all music albums that contain a *produced by* property connected to George Clinton, we would not get the same information that a query for "get all of the albums in George Clinton's record where he is listed as producer" would retrieve.

5. What terms in our ontology map directly to another ontology?

Chapter 3 demonstrated that entities describing the same object in different datasets could be connected with relationship designations. Likewise, ontologies can be connected to each other using properties to indicate comparable relationships. We can use ontologies on top of our existing data and controlled vocabularies to connect related information, express relationships between related datasets, and seamlessly extend dynamic webs of knowledge to researchers that they can then use to better understand their topic with much more valuable context.

INTERLINKING TO OTHER SEMANTIC DATA
AND INFERENCING INFORMATION

In chapter 3, our data model included linking our *Mothership Connection* entity to the same object in TuneEggheadz, a (fake) semantic database about music. Here, we will use the aforementioned Music Ontology (MO), an extensive (real-life) semantic database of concepts describing recorded sound and music releases. Since our example data model contains some overlapping information, we can look for places where our properties, classes, and individuals match up and then make those connections explicit with relationship properties.

Figure 4.2 describes the areas in which TuneEggheadz and MO overlap. Because our dataset is built to describe objects held by our library, it will likely contain a considerable amount of information related specifically to those objects and the library's typical administration of those items (local identifier, storage locations, and so on), which does not apply to the MO in any meaningful way.

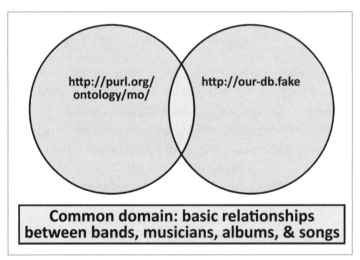

FIGURE 4.2
Diagram of the "common domain" between
TuneEggheadz and Music Ontology

However, both ontologies contain the basic descriptions and relationships of bands, musicians, albums, and songs. This is called the *common knowledge domain*, the area where ontology designers ensure interoperability with other ontologies. Instead of covering all music-related topics within our ontology, we can leverage their framework while we work on more specific description.

Our data model contains the property *produced by* (*prop004*), connected to our entity representing George Clinton. As it happens, a similar property exists in the MO ontology: *producer* (*http://purl.org/ontology/mo/producer*). Since these properties represent the same concept—a person or group entity that was responsible for shaping the sound of the album's recording—they can be connected. Figure 4.3 shows that our *produced by* property has been connected to *equivalent property*, a property found in the Web Ontology Language (OWL), which was created in 2004 and is now maintained and published by the W3C as a recommended Semantic Web standard. *Equivalent property* denotes alikeness between ontologies, and is heavily used to link between ontologies and datasets.

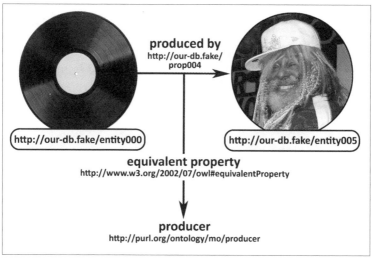

FIGURE 4.3
Diagram of "produced by" property

You may be wondering how linking data guarantees wider enrichment and discovery. The short answer is: it doesn't. Providing links to other ontologies and entities does not automatically mean that a user will be inundated with information from other sources. The actual connections are made via semantic agents, similar to the web crawlers and indexers of search engines like Google or DuckDuckGo. We have to trust that our ontology design will make it easy for machine-driven crawlers to understand our connections.

Of course, there are never any guarantees in web-based indexing, so some graphs attempt to achieve maximum interlinking by directly using properties from other ontologies. Figure 4.4 shows our example with OWL's *equivalent property* dispensed entirely, replaced with the direct property URI of MO's

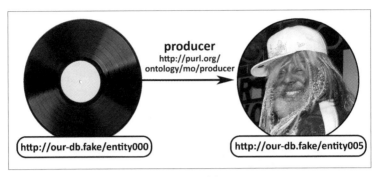

FIGURE 4.4
Diagram of "producer" property

producer. But we can take this further and replace even more of the properties we initially created in chapter 3, replacing them with properties from core RDF ontologies mentioned earlier. After substituting the MO property for ours, a Turtle serialization of our data looks like this:

```
@prefix odb: <http://our-db.fake/> .
@prefix eggheadz: <http://tuneeggheadz.fake/> .
@prefix mo: <http://purl.org/ontology/mo/> .

odb:entity000
   odb:prop001 odb:entity001 ;
   odb:prop002 "NBLP 7022" ;
   odb:prop003 odb:entity003 ;
   mo:producer odb:entity005 ;
   odb:prop005 odb:entity006 ;
   odb:prop006 eggheadz:byz6wd .
```

At the time, it made sense for us to create a property that would allow us to identify *Mothership Connection* as a type of music album (*prop001*). However, that particular relationship is already defined in RDFS as the property rdf: type. In fact, it's so often used in linked data, that the Turtle format simply uses the letter a as shorthand for a triple property indicating type:

```
odb:entity000
   a odb:entity001 ;
```

We can also remove our special property used to indicate that our *Mothership Connection* node was the same as the one found in TuneEggheadz (*prop005*). That particular relationship is also already well covered, this time by *owl:sameAs*, which links similar individual nodes together. From there, we can continue looking for other places where other ontologies can substitute for our in-house properties:

```
@prefix odb: <http://our-db.fake/> .
@prefix eggheadz: <http://tuneeggheadz.fake/> .
@prefix mo: <http://purl.org/ontology/mo/> .
@prefix rdf: <http://www.w3.org/1999/02/22-rdf-syntax-ns#> .
@prefix owl: <http://www.w3.org/2002/07/owl#> .

odb:entity000
  a mo:album ;
  mo:catalogue_number "NBLP 7022" ;
  odb:prop003 odb:entity003 ;
  mo:producer odb:entity005 ;
  odb:prop005 odb:entity006 ;
  owl:sameAs eggheadz:byz6wd .
```

Some readers may wonder why we went to the trouble of making properties if other, more popular relationship terms already existed. The point of all of this was to demonstrate that linked data, as a concept, is not just about focusing on connecting our *Mothership Connection* node to the imaginary TuneEggheadz node; linked data is also about leveraging common languages *within* data so that everyone is speaking a common—if not exactly the same—language.

The usefulness of speaking a common language is exemplified by *inferencing*, or drawing conclusions from semantically linked data by way of computer processing. Inferencing allows users to work with data from more than one dataset by applying logic to triple statements and ontological connections. Take, for example, our *Mothership Connection* node, which is connected to the same entity in the TuneEggheadz dataset; our local semantic information about the album is pretty bare-bones. However, if the TuneEggheadz node is linked to other *Mothership Connection* nodes in other semantic datasets, then the triple statements of those connections could be inferred as statements that also represent *our* node. Figure 4.5 illustrates this situation; assuming that

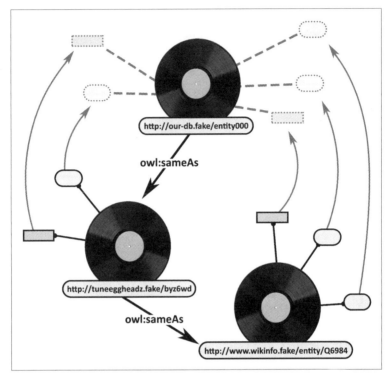

FIGURE 4.5
Diagram of inferred RDF data

each node is semantically notated as being the same as another, a computer could logically climb through each node, collect its triples, and infer that those statements must also apply to *our* node. These statements could be compiled and displayed to the user, or even be added to our node to fill in gaps. The possibilities presented by the systematic processing and discovery of information is what makes linked data more than just a new and shiny method of encoding information.[15]

ONTOLOGICAL PROBLEMS

Ontologies depend upon precise definitions and a deep understanding of the context in a given domain. This means that their usefulness depends on content experts trusting and finding value in the ways that ontologies express what is known in the field. Content contributors—both subject experts and ontology designers—have a very important role to play in developing, assessing, and encouraging the adoption of ontologies by communities, including the GLAM community. Shared knowledge, as reflected in an adopted ontology, is critical to accurate results and the overall impressions of the technology's value.

Currently, there's no single place where ontologies are described or documented. This means that we cannot think of linked data as an off-the-shelf product, but rather as a set of ingredients that can be combined in a recipe to create different structured data products. One of the challenges for linked data in practice is understanding how the concepts of ontologies are being used and adopted among various communities. Because this work in libraries is relatively new, the library profession has an opportunity to engage in the conversation about ontology development, encourage the reuse of existing ontologies, and identify unmet needs that demand attention and problem-solving.

Ontologies are also human resource-intensive. Though there are many automated ways to build and augment ontologies, constructing and maintaining them take a significant amount of (human) intellectual work. There is still need for a common infrastructure and the sharing of priorities and outcomes. Due to the nature of multiple disciplines working on the same challenges, it would be beneficial to identify cross-pollination and collaboration opportunities that bring together the experience of information professionals, metadata specialists, computer scientists, ontology designers, and system architects. Through an approach that recognizes the various experiences and common goals of these library-inclusive (and adjacent) professions, ontologies would benefit and confusion in terminology could be overcome.

Another problem is that ontology adoption rates are difficult to calculate, and ontologies themselves can be changed or applied to varying degrees. There are several governance bodies working in communities using ontologies and Semantic Web architectures that can help oversee and counteract the open nature of ontologies, but this is an issue to be aware of, since even in the same domain, no two ontologies will be the same, and reuse should be encouraged versus creating a new ontology.

As we close out this section, the most important thing to take away is that ontologies help us invest in our data. They give us a tool to endow our knowledge with the rich description we value most, as well as the hidden context between items within the data. They offer librarians—as creators, contributors, users, and consumers of knowledge—a way to be leaders in adding value to users of libraries of the future.

By understanding when to seek out and apply an ontology, our community becomes an active participant in delivering our local information to users of a hyper-connected and dynamic new world of data.

NOTES

1. Daniel Palzer, "Ontology-Based Services in Multi-Agent Systems" (Diploma thesis, University of Porto, Portugal, 2005), https://web.fe.up.pt/~eol/SOCRATES/Palzer/ontologies.htm.
2. Thomas R. Gruber, "Toward Principles for the Design of Ontologies Used for Knowledge Sharing?" *International Journal of Human-Computer Studies* 43 no. 5–6 (November 1995): 908.
3. Willem Nico Borst, "Construction of Engineering Ontologies" (PhD thesis, Institute for Telematica and Information Technology, University of Twente, Netherlands, 1997), 12.
4. Joseph T. Tennis and Javier Calzada-Prado, "Ontologies and the Semantic Web: Problems and Perspectives for LIS Professionals," *Ibersid* 12 (2007): 1.
5. David Stuart, "Library and Information Professionals: Builders of the Ontological Universe," *Information Today,* last modified January 1, 2014, www.thefreelibrary.com/Library+and+information+professionals%3A+builders+of+the+ontological+...-a0360995275.
6. World Wide Web Consortium, Standards, "Ontologies," www.w3.org/standards/semanticweb/ontology.
7. Dieter Fensel, *Ontologies: A Silver Bullet for Knowledge Management and Electronic Commerce* (London: Springer, 2004), 5–6.
8. Europeana, "Europeana Data Model Primer," last modified July 14, 2013, https://pro.europeana.eu/files/Europeana_Professional/Share_your_data/Technical_requirements/EDM_Documentation/EDM_Primer_130714.pdf.
9. Namespaces available at www.w3.org/1999/02/22-rdf-syntax-ns# and www.w3.org/2000/01/rdf-schema#, respectively.
10. World Wide Web Consortium, "RDF Schema 1.1," last modified February 25, 2014, www.w3.org/TR/rdf-schema/.
11. Tim Berners-Lee, "Giant Global Graph." Decentralized Information Group, Massachusetts Institute of Technology, last modified November 21, 2007, archived from the original at https://web.archive.org/web/20160713021037/ and http://dig.csail.mit.edu/breadcrumbs/node/215.
12. "Ontology: a formal model that allows knowledge to be represented for a specific domain. An ontology describes the types of things that exist (classes), the relationships between them (properties), and the logical ways those classes and properties can be used together (axioms)," World Wide Web Consortium, www.w3.org/TR/ld-glossary.
13. Sebastian Ryszard Kruk and Bill McDaniel, eds., *Semantic Digital Libraries* (London: Springer, 2009), 42.
14. Kruk and McDaniel, *Semantic Digital Libraries,* 43–44.
15. Ruth Kitchin Tillman, "Barriers to Ethical Name Modeling in Current Linked Data Encoding Practices," in *Ethical Questions in Name Authority Control,* ed. Jane Sandberg (Sacramento, CA: Library Juice, 2019), 247–48.

ONCE UPON A TIME CALLED NOW

Real-World Examples of Linked Data

Picture, if you will, the blank search box of your preferred internet search engine. You can't recall which streaming service has the rights to Marvel's 2018 superhero film *Black Panther*, but with any luck, that information will be somewhere near the top of the results. Your fingers type out your search, hit "return," and hope for the best. . . .

Variations on the above scenario have long been a staple for evangelists of linked data. The scenarios usually invoke a hypothetical web search for a popular car named after an animal (Jaguars, Mustangs, Impalas), and the search results inevitably contain both automobiles and wildlife. As you know by now, the World Wide Web was (and still is) a gigantic collection of files. Some of them are pictures, but most are souped-up text files, and the problem was, no matter how powerful the search engines' algorithms, search results were still unreliable. After all, web crawlers weren't smart enough to make sense of the web data they were consuming; they simply looked for text that matched the search query and then returned the most clicked-on result. What if, the evangelists asked, someday web crawlers could use linked data to differentiate between a query for a sports car and a search for information on an animal?

Since then, search algorithms have evolved and become exponentially better, albeit with new kinds of unreliability. A search for "black panther" will lead Google's search algorithm to make a reasoned assumption that you are looking for information about the ninth-highest-grossing motion picture ever—not the animal, not the comic books the movie is based on, and not the 1960s political organization. Change your search to "black panther animal" and, unsurprisingly, you'll get different results about big cats with less conflated results and fewer false positives—provided you started with the right search terms.

Search quality isn't the only thing that's changed. Different search engines have their own idiosyncrasies, but both Google and Bing now augment their results by generating "infoboxes" that contain basic and supplemental information related to a search. (Google's version is referred to as the Knowledge Graph Panel; Bing's is called the Snapshot Pane.) Figure 5.1 contains Knowledge Graph Card examples generated from two different "black panther" queries; in both cases, the search engine intuitively understands the requests and returned unambiguous information about specific topics.

What's changed about web searches? The short answer is: linked data is being used to disambiguate search queries. Instead of relying solely on an index of text consumed from web-crawling, Google announced in 2012 that it had instituted the Knowledge Graph, a database housing millions of facts and interconnected metadata chunks, pieced together from web sources that Google had already consumed and indexed. When a Google search matches a node in the Knowledge Graph, it returns not only the most closely associated web results, but basic facts (i.e., triples) via a Knowledge Graph Card.

One of the most common complaints when learning about linked data is the perceived lack of concrete examples. The assumption even of those librarians who advocate for the adoption and expansion of linked data and the Semantic Web in libraries—an assumption which is sometimes correct, and sometimes not—is that its benefits would be largely theoretical. This assumption may have been true in the years following the nascent discussions of the Semantic Web, but it no longer holds water—not for libraries, and certainly not for the tech industry as a whole. Chapter 6 covers some of the modern developments in linked library data, but if you're looking for solid examples of the Semantic Web permeating ordinary life, you needn't look further than the online tools and services you probably use every day.

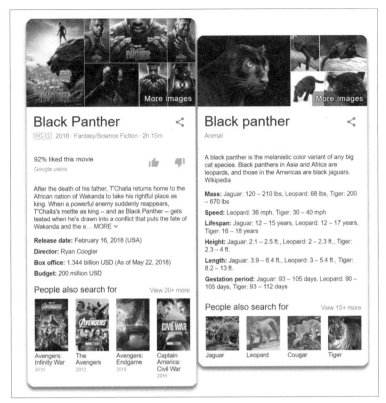

FIGURE 5.1
**Comparison of Google Knowledge Panels
from "black panther" searches**

OPEN GRAPH

If you use social media—and chances are you do, considering that about 2.5 billion people worldwide belong to some kind of social networking platform— then you are no doubt accustomed to the fact that content is often shared in different forms, predominantly text, video, images, and web links.[1] Facebook started as a kind of *social graph*—that is, a graph database storing information about which node (person) was connected to other nodes (people), which was not terribly dissimilar from the FOAF framework. As the site grew, it allowed users to share text-based posts, photos, and eventually video, all of which became nodes in the graph. Internally, detailed metadata could be added to these nodes, while externally, they could be shared, liked, and commented on as if they were Facebook pages representing local restaurants or businesses, making them *rich objects* in the graph.

This is useful, to a certain extent, for user-generated objects. URLs, on the other hand, suffer the same semantic issues we identified way back in chapter 1 —that is, a link by itself carries no inherent descriptive information unless the text of its HTML is parsed directly; and even then, the "aboutness" of a parsed web page can be iffy.

Enter Facebook's *Open Graph Protocol* (OGP).[2] Introduced in 2010, Open Graph offers a linked-data method for turning URLs into similar kinds of shareable objects in a social graph. If you were to paste the URL of George Clinton's official Parliament-Funkadelic website (www.georgeclinton.com) into a blank Facebook post, you would see something akin to figure 5.2. Facebook has automatically created a rich object—a thing that can be liked and shared—rather than just posting a plain-text URL into your post.

FIGURE 5.2
Facebook post featuring an open graph object

The object includes key information about George Clinton and Parliament-Funkadelic, including the website's title and description.

But how does Facebook construct these rich objects? As it turns out, the OGP was based on *RDFa*, a W3C extension of HTML5 (the latest version of the markup language used in the World Wide Web). RDFa (or *RDF Attributes*) was introduced to facilitate adding semantic data directly to the structure of HTML, turning the human-text content of web pages into computer-readable data without having to duplicate code or data for the computers.[3] (Side note: Does the situation of duplicating data for humans and computers in a single document remind you at all of MARC?) RDFa provides a limited set of HTML attributes that turn sections of the web page (or the web page as a whole) into RDF triples; the attributes themselves—like *about* and *typeof*—provide meaningful triple predicates about content in the HTML, connected to either URIs or literal objects. For example, a web designer might wrap the following code around the main content of a blog entry:

```
<div vocab="http://data.fake/">
       <div typeof="BlogPost">
       <h1><span property="hasTitle">Funky Life: On Linked
Data and "Mothership Connection"</span></h1>
</div>
```

The RDFa property "typeof" is actually a stand-in for the `rdf:type` property. So, when a web crawler comes along that is equipped for parsing RDFa, the code would communicate to the crawler that the content is an example of the *BlogPost* class, found in the ontology at `<http://data.fake/>`. (Figure 5.3 shows a diagram of this triple.)

Like RDFa, Open Graph utilizes the same mechanism: when URLs are dropped into social media objects, Facebook consumes the OGP-marked metadata and creates a rich object in its internal databases. Unlike RDFa, Open Graph markup is not added to the body content of a web page; instead, OGP data is entered in the `<head>` tag. If you were to connect to George Clinton's website in a browser and view its source HTML, you might see the following metadata near the top, which has been shortened and formatted for clarity's sake (see the following page):

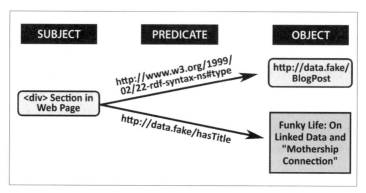

FIGURE 5.3
RDFa Diagram

```
<html lang="en-US" xmlns:"og: http://ogp.me/ns#"
itemscope itemtype="https://schema.org/WebPage">
<head>
        <meta property="og:locale" content="en_US" />
        <meta property="og:type" content="website" />
        <meta property="og:title" content="George Clinton
Parliament Funkadelic official website" />
        <meta property="og:description" content="Official site
of George Clinton and Parliament Funkadelic - Home of the
extraterrestrial brothers, Dealers of funky music P.Funk,
uncut funk, The Bomb" />
        <meta property="og:url" content="https://
georgeclinton.com" />
        <meta property="og:site_name" content="Official Website
of George Clinton Parliament Funkadelic" />
</head>
```

Right away, we can see some familiar structures; the `<head>` data contains what looks like a namespace declaration for the OGP. Sure enough, this is an ontology. As we saw with Turtle in chapter 3, this declaration turns every `meta property` value prefixed with `og:` into triple predicates; the `content` property values become literal objects. (Figure 5.4 shows a diagram of this triple.) The OGP-coded objects serve up the information that populates Facebook's rich objects, like title and descriptive data.

FIGURE 5.4
Open graph diagram

While the Open Graph Protocol is available through what has been referred to as "a considerably open license for a web standard written and controlled by one company," Facebook's internal graph is still closed.[4] Facebook consumes OGP metadata in website `<head>` tags but does not share the graph data made from that information, making OGP a tool of semantically acquired but not open data. Furthermore, the information the OGP trawls for is, more or less, just an extension of the `<meta>` tags that were abandoned by web crawlers and SEO (search engine optimization) specialists some time ago; no matter what the good intentions of its creators are, the OGP is still susceptible to spam and deceptive metadata problems, just as the `<meta>` tags were. Indeed, the Open Graph Protocol is designed to suck up just enough `<head>` metadata to create an object that looks clickable on a social media timeline, and that can include snake oil and misinformation just as it might include genuinely helpful or true information.

Spam and deceptive behavior are often kept in check on Facebook by security algorithms that track the behavior of individual users; if the algorithms see a pattern in behavior that has been previously identified as spammy or abusive, Facebook takes steps to disable or limit that account.[5] But what about sharing links that have questionable or misleading OGP metadata? In linked data, the credibility of information is attained (or, more likely, at least bolstered) by connecting things to other existing forms of the same things. We connected our *Mothership Connection* node to the same thing in the Tune-Eggheadz dataset in order to prove the accuracy and the existence of our node; a human being could look at both nodes and agree that they indeed describe the same thing, while a computer might collate and compare the data between the two, inferring accuracy between their triple statements. But when your triple objects rely on text meant for humans, bad actors don't have to worry as much about including accurate or truthful data because, as we have reiterated, human-readable text is difficult for computers to process. At the same time, social media companies don't necessarily feel compelled to worry about bad actors "gaming" (manipulating) their systems, since sharing links on their platforms is a major source of their revenue. If anyone ever tells you that linked data can't be used for disinformation or self-promotion, don't believe the hype.

SCHEMA.ORG

OGP isn't the only form of RDF embedded in the HTML of George Clinton's website. The first line of the HTML, which declares the kind of document with an <HTML> tag, also includes this piece of information:

```
<html ... itemscope itemtype="https://schema.org/WebPage">
```

This is an example of *Microdata*, a markup format similar to RDFa; while RDFa includes some built-in RDF properties for creating triples, Microdata strips that away, leaving the mechanism of representing triples without a specific ontology. Figure 5.5 shows a diagram of this triple. In this triple, itemscope creates a node for the <HTML> element, making the entire content of the web page the subject of a triple, while itemtype serves as its type property; here the webmaster has used Schema.org, a linked data ontology preferred by many web search engines. This Microdata triple accomplishes two things: first, putting itemscope within the document's HTML declaration means that any other following Microdata expressions in this web page will implicitly be information *about* this particular page; and second, the use of a specific ontology (schema.org) signals that any other Microdata triples about this web page will also use Schema.org as their namespace (unless other ontologies are explicitly declared).

What is Schema.org, you might ask? A year after the Open Graph Protocol debuted, the then-largest web aggregators in the world—Google, Microsoft, and

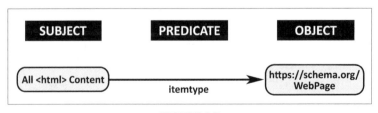

FIGURE 5.5
Schema.org diagram 1

Yahoo, later joined by the Russian-language search engine Yandex—launched their own markup schema for semantically describing web content. Fittingly titled Schema.org, the project proposed a set of structured ontologies that could be recognized and consumed by all search engine crawlers, with the added ability to extend its metadata beyond the most common types of internet content. This information (referred to nowadays as "structured data") is embedded in a web page's HTML code, which crawlers could consume, "understanding" the contents of the page. This kind of semantic parsing would play a part in how search results appeared to users—or, in the case of Google's Knowledge Graph, feed information directly into its knowledge base.

Given that Google dominates the world's market share of web searches, it is not unreasonable for us to look at Schema.org examples through the lens of Google's recommended usage.[6] Metadata marked up with Schema.org's linked data can be deployed with Microdata and RDFa, but Google recommends using JSON-LD.

CASE IN POINT
Schema.org in JSON-LD

If we wanted to construct a JSON-LD code block representing George Clinton's official Parliament-Funkadelic website, we could use what already exists in the <head> tag to create this JSON-LD object:

```
<script type="application/ld+json">
{

        "@context": "http://schema.org",
        "@type": "WebSite",
        "url": "https://www.georgeclinton.com/",
        "name": "George Clinton Parliament Funkadelic
Official Website",
        "description": "Official site of George Clinton
and Parliament Funkadelic - Home of the extraterrestrial
brothers, Dealers of funky music P.Funk, uncut funk, The
Bomb"
}
</script>
```

Like the Open Graph example, much of this content is literal text values, except `@type`. Recall from earlier that JSON-LD expects text, numbers, and booleans as values; by using `@type`, we're acknowledging that the value "WebSite" is going to be a URI (http://schema.org/WebSite), not text or numbers. (This is diagrammed in figure 5.6.) The implication here is that the actual website for George Clinton is the subject of the resulting triples; however, eagle-eyed readers will notice that our JSON-LD block doesn't actually identify a subject URI with the node identifier (`@id`). "Couldn't we create a URI representing Parliament and use that?" you may ask. The answer is ... complicated. Remember, the node identifier specifies the subject of our triples—in this case, the website for George Clinton and Parliament-Funkadelic. If we were to add a new URI here, we would be explicitly identifying that this linked data is about *the real-life George Clinton and Parliament-Funkadelic*, not *the website about George Clinton and Parliament-Funkadelic*. This distinction may seem pedantic, but remember, the point of linked data is to represent both knowledge and real-world entities as accurately as possible.

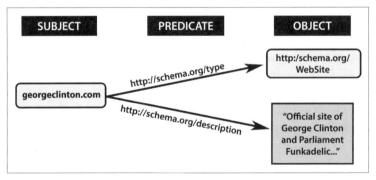

FIGURE 5.6
Schema.org diagram 2

That being said, there are a number of ways that we could identify both the JSON-LD subject as a website *and* connect it to real-world things. The example on the following page is one method.

```
<script type="application/ld+json">
{
        "@context": "http://schema.org",
        "@type": "WebSite",
        "@id": "https://www.georgeclinton.com/#website",
        "url": "https://www.georgeclinton.com/",
        "name": "George Clinton Parliament Funkadelic
Official Website",
        "description": "Official site of George Clinton
and Parliament Funkadelic - Home of the extraterrestrial
brothers, Dealers of funky music P.Funk, uncut funk, The
Bomb",
        "mainEntity": [
          {
            "@type": "Person",
            "name": "George Clinton",
            "@id": "http://our-db.fake/entity005"
          },
          {
            "@type": "MusicGroup",
            "name": "Parliament-Funkadelic",
            "@id": "http://our-db.fake/entity009"
          }
          ]
}
</script>
```

A couple of new things are going on here:

1. First, we've added a node identifier URI to the main block, *https://www.georgeclinton.com/#website*. In the world of linked data, this is known as a *hash URI*. Adding `#website` to the URL is intended to explicitly identify that the conceptual subject of the JSON-LD code is a website—not a URL and not the real-world entities George Clinton or Parliament-Funkadelic.

2. Second, we also added the Schema URI for schema.org/mainEntity. The `mainEntity` property allows us to explicitly identify the focus of a JSON-LD node identifier (in our case, the website). Our website is about both George Clinton and the current version of the Parliament-Funkadelic collective; consequently, we have two added two nodes to `mainEntity` representing both, and explicitly identifying them as a schema.org/Person and a schema.org/MusicalGroup, respectively. Each node is represented by a unique URI: for George Clinton, we use our existing node (entity005), and a new URI representing the P-Funk collective (entity009).

3. In a perfect world, the result would be that crawlers for Google (or some other web indexer) would come along and, using, our linked data, semantically understand that this is (a) a website about (b) George Clinton and (c) the Parliament-Funkadelic music collective.

DEEP DIVE
Representing Concert Data with JSON-LD

Schema.org data is not limited to just low-level information descriptive information about websites; its core vocabulary includes markup for creative works, embedded non-text objects (audio, images, video), events, places, organizations, people, products, reviews, and more. In addition, community-developed extensions have followed, allowing detailed knowledge areas like automotive and life science metadata to build on the core. (In chapter 6, we will look at how librarians extended Schema.org with an extension vocabulary for bibliographic description.) The real-life George Clinton/Parliament-Funkadelic website, for example, *does* include a small amount of JSON-flavored linked data: impending performance dates encoded with Schema.org properties. Ordinarily, this kind of information would need to be parsed by web crawlers from HTML, but the embedded JSON-LD objects are rich with semantic data:

```json
{
        "@context": "http://schema.org",
        "@type": "MusicEvent",
        "name": "George Clinton & Parliament Funkadelic @
Catch One",
        "startDate": "2018-12-15T19:00:00",
        "url": "https://www.bandsintown.com/e/1012507124?app
_id=js_georgeclinton.com&came_from=242&utm_medium=api&utm
_source=public_api&utm_campaign=event",
        "location": {
                "@type": "Place",
                "name": "Catch One",
                "address": {
                        "@type": "PostalAddress",
                        "addressCountry": "United States",
                        "addressRegion": "CA",
                        "addressLocality": "Los Angeles"
                },
                "geo": {
                        "@type": "GeoCoordinates",
                        "latitude": "34.047827",
                        "longitude": "-118.324115"
                }
        },
        "performers": [
                {
                "@type": "MusicGroup",
                "name": "George Clinton & Parliament
Funkadelic"
                }
        ]
}
```

Schema.org can be found in millions of websites, but like Open Graph, it's ultimately another example of (mostly) closed-world linked data; post-harvest, Google doesn't expose much of its Knowledge Graph data to outside queries, apart from basic descriptive information. A query into Google's Knowledge Graph for its George Clinton node produces a block of schema.org-encoded JSON-LD (see the following page):

```
{
    "@context": {
        "@vocab": "http://schema.org/",
        "goog": "http://schema.googleapis.com/",
        "EntitySearchResult": "goog:EntitySearchResult",
        "detailedDescription": "goog:detailedDescrip tion",
        "resultScore": "goog:resultScore",
        "kg": "http://g.co/kg"
    },
    "@type": "ItemList",
    "itemListElement": [
        {
            "@type": "EntitySearchResult",
            "result": {
            "@id": "kg:/m/0ql36",
            "name": "George Clinton",
            "@type": [
                "Person",
                "Thing"
            ],
            "description": "American singer",
            "detailedDescription": {
                "articleBody": "George Edward Clinton is
an American singer, songwriter, bandleader, and record
producer. His Parliament-Funkadelic collective developed
an influential and eclectic form of funk music during the
1970s that drew on science-fiction, outlandish fashion,
psychedelic culture, and surreal humor."
            } [. . .]
```

Once semantic information is funneled into the interior data coffers of private companies, how that information is used and stored remains a mystery to all of us on the outside. To be honest, this is hardly the fault of Google or Facebook alone; as the Dutch coder Hay Kranen points out, webmasters are expected to use these tools to capitalize on good-looking social media posts and raise their SEO profiles, not to help realize a practical implementation of data publishing.[7] Nevertheless, the curious rebranding of these concepts as "structured data"—instead of linked or semantic data—seems like an indicator of the difficulty in creating a web of open information.

Back in 2010, Tim Berners-Lee updated his 2006 Linked Data post to include a star-based rating system to encourage the web community—"especially government data owners"—to create not just linked data, but *linked open data*, or linked data released under an open license for free reuse. While there's nothing inherently wrong with a private company maintaining a private graph of semantic information, Berners-Lee's star rating system shows how linked data becomes progressively more powerful as more people can use it:

> **One Star:** Data is available on the web in no fixed format, but has an open license.
>
> **Two Stars:** Same as One Star, but the data is machine-readable and structured, such as a spreadsheet instead of a JPEG image of a data table.
>
> **Three Stars:** All of the above, plus the data is made available in a nonproprietary format, such as a tab-separated or comma-separated file instead of an Excel spreadsheet.
>
> **Four Stars:** All of the above, plus the data is made available with semantic standards, like RDF, fulfilling Berners-Lee's first three rules of linked data (see chapter 3).
>
> **Five Stars:** All of the above, plus the data is connected to other open datasets.[8]

Projects that make human knowledge available as linked, open data now number in the thousands. Two specific examples of 5-Star Linked Open Data projects will serve as the final examples of this chapter.

DBPEDIA

If you're already familiar with Google and Facebook, then odds are you're also familiar with *Wikipedia*. Launched in 2001, this online, noncommercial encyclopedia is alternately lauded for its worldwide access to open knowledge and rightly criticized for the systemic bias and sexism not only in its notability guidelines for content, but in the editorial choices made by its volunteer content editors. Regardless, as of 2019, *Wikipedia* was the eighth-most visited website in the world, and the encyclopedia has more than 5.9 million articles in

English alone.[9] This enormous knowledge base could be a boon to researchers worldwide, but the prose-based style of encyclopedia content, along with the fact that *Wikipedia*'s use of infoboxes is "neither required nor prohibited for any article," has hampered attempts to make its data graphable.[10]

An attempt to remedy this situation came in 2007 with the release of the first version of *DBpedia*. Formed by members of the Free University of Berlin and Leipzig University, DBpedia is a crowd-sourced linked data translation of *Wikipedia*, with the bulk of its content extracted from structured data—such as its infoboxes, category metadata, and links to other websites—found in projects made by the Wikimedia Foundation, *Wikipedia*'s parent organization. The resulting semantic dataset is made accessible through open licenses (the Creative Commons CC-BY-SA License and the GNU Free Documentation License), allowing pretty much anyone to reuse the dataset.

DBpedia was created in collaboration with a company called OpenLink Software, known for its Virtuoso, an open-source software platform that combines multiple components—like triplestores and web servers—needed to deploy linked data. DBpedia's RDF data is hosted and published using Virtuoso,

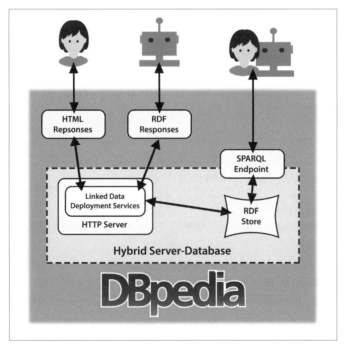

FIGURE 5.7
Content negotiation diagram

which in turn handles all human- and machine-generated data queries. Many of these data requests involve a human looking for the entire record of a single thing in the triplestore—or, in the case of scripted code, many records, one right after another. Web browsers like Chrome and Firefox automatically send instructions with these requests, telling Virtuoso that the user is expecting it to return a human-readable version of the record. A script or a semantic web crawler, on the other hand, will probably want a machine-readable version of the same record, which the server can return if asked correctly (and nicely). This strategy—in which a triplestore or a web server delivers different kinds of semantic data depending on the type of user requesting it—is called *content negotiation*, and it ensures that you get the kind of linked data you're expecting to see from the server. (See figure 5.7 for an illustration.)

CASE IN POINT
Content Negotiation and DBpedia

Consider DBpedia's translation of the *Wikipedia* article on the Parliament-Funkadelic music collective (https://en.wikipedia.org/wiki/Parliament-Funkadelic). The URI for the DBpedia version is wholly based on the *Wikipedia* URL: http://dbpedia.org/resource/Parliament-Funkadelic. Depending on how this URI is accessed, the Virtuoso server assesses the incoming request and decides which version to send back:

1. If we try to access the URI from a web browser, what comes back to us is a new URI—http://dbpedia.org/page/Parliament-Funkadelic, an HTML representation of the raw linked data. This web page is sparse—in fact, it's mostly a list of the raw data points—but it's formatted for us humans to read.
2. If we were to send the correct instructions to the server, we could just as easily get back either RDF/XML, JSON-LD, Turtle. or N-Triple representations of the same Parliament-Funkadelic record. (*Note:* Scenario 2 can also be sent through a web browser; for example, the Turtle representation of the Parliament-Funkadelic data can be found at http://dbpedia.org/data/Parliament-Funkadelic.ttl, the N-Triples version at http://dbpedia.org/data/Parliament-Funkadelic.ntriples, and so on.)

The above example covers the retrieval of single records, but what if we wanted to search all of DBpedia for a single kind of information that might be referenced in lots of records? What if, for example, we wanted to look through all of DBpedia to find the titles of funk albums that were released in 1975? How would we go about querying the entire graph to find this information?

DEEP DIVE
SPARQLing DBpedia

Recall that in chapter 3, we mentioned SPARQL, a Semantic Web tool that is used to query vast amounts of RDF data. DBpedia offers a *SPARQL endpoint*, or a kind of gateway that processes SPARQL queries and retrieves the results from its graph, at https://dbpedia.org/sparql. Upon arrival, you will see that DBpedia has been selected as our target graph; below that is an empty box where we will construct our SPARQL query.

There are many different kinds of SPARQL queries—for example, we could ask True/False questions based on what's in the graph, or we can even send queries that would write new data to it. The most common type is a SELECT query, which tells the server that we are requesting specific chunks of data from its triplestore. Since we need to ask specific questions about a large volume of data, we will ask those questions with variables, or temporary stand-ins for the specific chunks of data. But first, we need to know how to ask those questions.

A SPARQL query returns triples from a triplestore, so it stands to reason that the query can, like the data itself, be read as a sentence. For example, it's fair to assume that DBpedia has enough information to be able to describe a particular item from the sentence: "*Mothership Connection* is a funk album by Parliament that was released on December 15, 1975." We can substitute DBpedia URIs into this statement like so:

> [http://dbpedia.org/resource/Mothership_Connection] **is a** [http://dbpedia.org/resource/Funk] [http://dbpedia.org/ontology/Album] **by** [http://dbpedia.org/resource/Parliament_(band)] **that was** [http://dbpedia.org/ontology/releaseDate] on [1975-12-15].

The question we want to ask is: what else was going on in the funk music landscape that year? We can take out some of the DBpedia URIs and substitute variables for the things we don't yet know:

> [**album_name**] is a [http://dbpedia.org/resource/Funk] [http://dbpedia.org/ontology/Album] by [**artist**] that was [http://dbpedia.org/ontology/releaseDate] on [**release date,** which should fall between 1975-01-01 and 1975-12-31].

So, our SPARQL query will:

1. Look for all DBpedia items that are classified as music albums;
2. Select only those results that are also classified as being funk music; and
3. Further filter those results to return only the albums that have a release date sometime in 1975.

Our SPARQL query might look like this:

```
01 PREFIX dbo: <http://dbpedia.org/ontology/>
02 PREFIX dbr: <http://dbpedia.org/resource/>
03 PREFIX foaf: <http://xmlns.com/foaf/0.1/>

04 SELECT ?band ?album_name ?released WHERE {
05 ?album rdf:type dbo:Album ;
06     dbo:genre dbr:Funk ;
07     foaf:name ?album_name ;
08     dbo:artist ?artist ;
09     dbo:releaseDate ?released .
10 ?artist foaf:name ?band .
11 FILTER (?released >= "1975-01-01"^^xsd:dateTime
  && ?released <= "1975-12-31"^^xsd:dateTime)
12 }
```

Let's break this query into component lines:

1. The query begins with three lines of PREFIX (i.e., namespace) declarations; we will use the DBpedia ontology (dbo), the graph of DBpedia items (dbr), and the Friend-of-a-Friend (foaf) ontology.
2. Line 4 tells the SPARQL endpoint that we are requesting specific chunks of data. Specifically, we are looking for the variables ?band, ?album_name, and ?released, which will be constructed through instructions delivered in the WHERE block of lines 5 through 11. (Notice that these instructions contain the punctuation of Turtle syntax.)
3. Lines 5 through 9 contain multiple instructions for DBpedia predicate-object pairs, all which pertain to a variable called ?album:
   a. First, it sets up the variable, in which we search for any DBpedia object with a classification (from rdf:type) set to the ontology value Album (dbo:Album).

b. It then selects only the albums where the DBpedia ontology property for Genre (dbo:genre) is connected to the item for Funk music (dbr:Funk), leaving a list of URIs of funk albums.

c. Then, it queries those funk albums to get literal text value for their titles (foaf:name), which will be saved as a new variable, ?album_name.

d. Those funk albums will likely be linked to the artists who recorded them; a list of URIs for these artists (from dbo:artist) will be set to the variable ?artist.

e. Finally, we grab the text value of the day each album was released (from dbo:releaseDate) to another new variable, ?released.

4. Line 10 returns to our list of artists (?artist) and retrieves the literal text value for each band's name—also stored in those records with foaf:name—as another new variable, ?band.

5. The final line of the query filters everything we have collected, looking for release dates that lie between January 1 and December 31 of 1975; anything outside of this scope is discarded, and the three variables we asked for are returned as a table.

At the time this SPARQL query was written, this was the result:

BAND	ALBUM_NAME	RELEASED
Parliament@en	Chocolate City@en	1975-04-08
Parliament@en	Mothership Connection@en	1975-12-15
War@en	Why Can't We Be Friends?@en	1975-06-16
The Temptations@en	A Song for You@en	1975-01-16
Earth, Wind & Fire@en	That's the Way of the World@en	1975-03-15
Sly Stone@en	High on You@en	1975-11-08
KC and the Sunshine Band@en	KC and the Sunshine Band@en	1975-07-06
Earth, Wind & Fire@en	Gratitude@en	1975-11-11
The Isley Brothers@en	The Heat Is On@en	1975-06-07
Ohio Players@en	Honey@en	1975-08-16

Note that this does not imply these were the only funk albums released that year; our SPARQL query has only returned all of the DBpedia resources that matched a set of criteria. If the resource has not been added to DBpedia or is missing one of these values, it will not be returned for this search; likewise, if we queried the band or album name with the `rdfs:label` property instead of `foaf:name`, we could potentially have received entirely different results!

With its open licensing and tools for anyone to use, it's incredibly difficult to overstate how critical DBpedia's impact has been on the web of linked, open data. As figure 5.8 on the following page illustrates, in 2007, the maintainers of the Linked Open Data Cloud—a diagram tracking connections between all known semantic ontologies—showed only 12 known datasets; a decade later, the diagram contains more than 1,200 datasets, with DBpedia's 9.5 billion triples situated as one of the beating hearts of the Semantic Web.[11] In addition, the magnitude of DBpedia's knowledge base led to its being one of the foundational datasets in projects like IBM's Watson (the artificial intelligence system which famously competed on *Jeopardy!*) and in Apple's disembodied iOS assistant Siri. (In fact, DBpedia still serves as a focal point for artificial intelligence and machine learning research.)

WIKIDATA

It wasn't long before other linked, open-data translations of *Wikipedia* began popping up, and the most logical host for one of these projects was the Wikimedia Foundation. Released in 2012 with major updates the following year, *Wikidata* tracked many of the same basic functions as DBpedia: both projects established URIs for entities found in *Wikipedia* content, and provide RDF data about those entities. But when you venture into the weeds, those paths diverge.

DBpedia focuses on generating linked data from infoboxes and internal links found on *Wikipedia* pages, with content updates and data corrections being coordinated by both volunteers and automated services. And because it is a direct translation of *Wikipedia*, the systemic racial and gender bias found in *Wikipedia*'s content—partly the result of punishingly exact notability guidelines, and partly due to the cultural demographic (i.e., white males) that has both the free time and the inclination to create and edit *Wikipedia* articles—was inescapably bequeathed to DBpedia.

Wikidata, on the other hand, acts as a centralized hub *for* Wikimedia projects, and is open to virtually anyone to actively edit. Wikidata touts a more

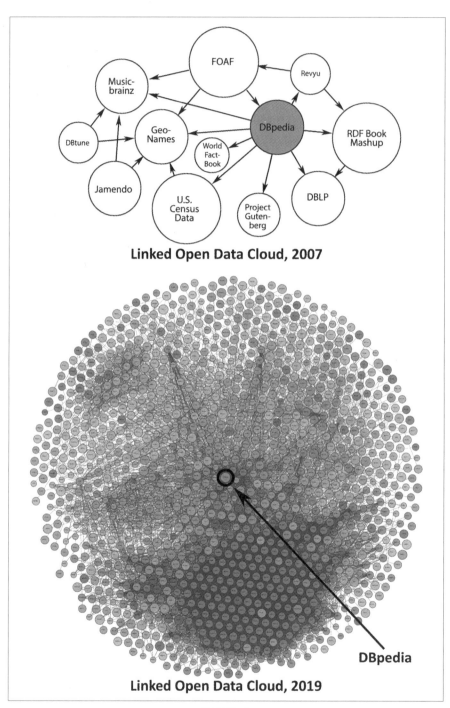

Linked Open Data Cloud, 2007

DBpedia

Linked Open Data Cloud, 2019

FIGURE 5.8
Linked open data cloud comparison

lenient approach to the scope of its content than its cousin, *Wikipedia*; if a real-world item doesn't have a link to a Wikimedia project in any language, but does describe "a clearly identifiable conceptual or material entity" using "serious and publicly available references," it's considered fair game.[12] This, along with a Creative Commons CC0 Public Domain license, creates the potential to extend Wikidata's usage beyond the scope of serving the Wikimedia projects and into the territory of an open, general knowledge base. (In fact, by the end of 2018, just over 27 million, or 51 percent, of all items in Wikidata carried no links to *Wikipedia* or other Wikimedia projects.)[13]

Wikidata assigns a unique identifier to its *items* (nodes) using numbers prefixed with the letter *Q* (a "QID"), allowing its URI to exist without favoring a specific language. Items are connected to each other via a Wikidata-specific property ontology, signified by a unique identifier prefixed with the letter *P* (a "PID"). Predicate-object pairs (which Wikidata refers to as *statements*) can be further qualified with references to validate the statement.

DEEP DIVE
Comparing Data Models

DBpedia's data model is *cross-domain*, meaning that a given record might contain more descriptive elements than just its own ontologies. Figure 5.9 on the following page shows a visualization of a select number of triples from the DBpedia record for Bootsy Collins, the longtime bassist of Parliament, Funkadelic, and other P-Funk family groups. DBpedia explicitly references external schemas like Dublin Core, FOAF, RDF, and OWL as both properties and items that describe Collins.

Wikidata's model is less transparent, predominantly referencing other Wikidata items and properties, as shown in figure 5.10 on the following page. However, both prop-erties and items can be linked to external ontologies using P1709 (*Equivalent Class*) and P1628 (*Equivalent Property*). In figure 5.8, one of Collins's occupations (*P106*) is singer (*Q177220*); in Wikidata, P106 is linked to similar concepts in Schema.org and the Library of Congress MADS standard, while "singer" is connected to an identical term in DBpedia. Similarly, Collins is an instance (*P31*) of a human (*Q5*), which is equivalent to nodes used by Schema .org and DBpedia.

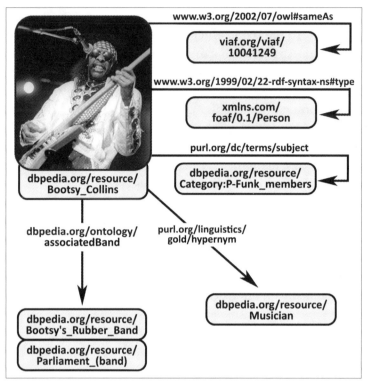

FIGURE 5.9
DBpedia diagram of Bootsy Collins

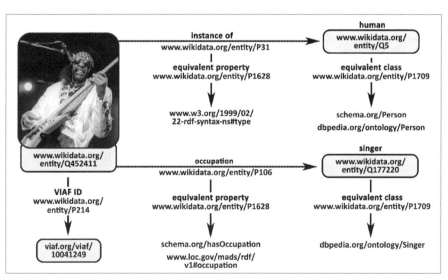

FIGURE 5.10
Wikidata diagram of Bootsy Collins

CASE IN POINT
SPARQLing Wikidata

Despite such ontological differences, Wikidata offers many of the same features as DBpedia, including a SPARQL endpoint—rebranded as the "Wikidata Query Service"—located at https://query.wikidata.org/.

We can use much of the same SPARQL syntax as our DBpedia example, albeit with a few changes. Since all of our data is specified within Wikidata's ontology, there is no need to declare namespaces for external properties; Wikidata's SPARQL will automatically know that the wdt prefix indicates a property URI (beginning with http://www.wikidata.org/prop/direct/), while wd is used to signify a Wikidata node URI (http://www.wikidata.org/entity/). Also, recall that in our previous query, we created several variables so we could grab item labels and store them as ?artist and ?album_name. Wikidata's endpoint includes a "label service" that automatically fetches an item's label, slightly reducing the complexity needed for our query. We add this with a SERVICE command after FILTER indicating a preference for English:

```
SELECT ?artistLabel ?albumLabel ?released WHERE {
?album wdt:P31 wd:Q482994;
       wdt:P136 wd:Q164444;
       wdt:P175 ?artist;
       wdt:P577 ?released.
FILTER (?released >= "1975-01-01"^^xsd:dateTime
       && ?released <=
       "1975-12-31"^^xsd:dateTime)
SERVICE wikibase:label { bd:serviceParam wikibase:language
"en". }
}
```

You may notice that as we construct this query, the "Query Helper" widget next to the SPARQL console automatically generates a dropdown-menu version of your query as you work. (See figure 5.11 on the following page.) This can serve to validate your efforts as you learn the SPARQL language, as well as assist you in creating new SPARQL queries for Wikidata.

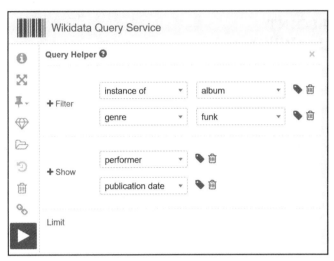

FIGURE 5.11
Wikidata Query Service screenshot

At the time this SPARQL query was written, this was the result:

ARTISTLABEL	ALBUMLABEL	RELEASED
Commodores	Caught in the Act	1 February 1975
Curtis Mayfield	Let's Do It Again	1 January 1975
Funkadelic	Let's Take It to the Stage	01 July 1975
Kool & the Gang	Spirit of the Boogie	01 August 1975
Parliament	Mothership Connection	01 January 1975
Rufus	Rufus featuring Chaka Khan	18 November 1975
The Natural Four	Heaven Right Here on Earth	01 January 1975
The People's Choice	Boogie Down U.S.A.	01 January 1975
Tower of Power	Urban Renewal	01 January 1975

Compare these results to our DBpedia results—the only overlapping entity is, ironically, *Mothership Connection*. Again, the differences are down to (1) whether the queried information is present in records, and (2) how albums are classified with respect to genre. For instance, in the *Wikipedia* article for Parliament's album *Chocolate City*, the infobox contains the genre tag for funk music; consequently, this data point was passed on to the DBpedia record. However, a genre classification is missing entirely in Wikidata. It just goes to show you that the integrity of your data analysis is only as good as the quality of your linked data!

So far, Wikidata seems to have been a resounding success story of linked data. In 2014, just two years after Wikidata's debut, the Open Data Institute—a nonprofit organization cofounded by Tim Berners-Lee—awarded the project the institute's first Open Data Publisher Award "for sheer scale, and built-in openness."[14] That same year, Google announced the sunsetting of another knowledge base project, Freebase. Google had acquired Freebase in 2010, and it soon became a primary source of the Knowledge Graph. However, in December 2014, Google announced that as Freebase prepared for an eventual shutdown, they would instead migrate Freebase's data to Wikidata, writing: "They're growing fast, have an active community, and are better-suited to lead an open collaborative knowledge base."[15] By Google's own account, the migration may have boosted Wikidata to the tune of approximately 19 million statements and identifiers.[16]

The growth of linked open data projects, including DBpedia and Wikidata, suggests a motivation to create that web of semantic data beyond the usual suspects—which, of course, includes librarians like you. But where, at this point, *are* libraries and archives when it comes to the Semantic Web? The next chapter investigates the state of linked data in the library and archives world.

NOTES

1. Statista, "Social Media Usage Worldwide," www.statista.com/study/12393/social-net works-statista-dossier/.
2. The Open Graph Protocol, http://ogp.me/.
3. World Wide Web Consortium, "HTML+RDFa 1.1: Support for RDFa in HTML4 and HTML5," last modified March 17, 2015, www.w3.org/TR/html-rdfa/.
4. Indiewebcamp, "The Open Graph Protocol," last modified April 30, 2019, https:// indieweb.org/The-Open-Graph-protocol.
5. "Using information from your reports and what we know about how the average person uses Facebook, we've identified certain common patterns of unacceptable behavior. For example, we've learned that if someone sends the same message to 50 people not on his or her friend list in the span of an hour, it's usually spam. Similarly, if 75 percent of the friend requests a person sends are ignored, it's very likely that that person is annoying others he or she doesn't actually know." Facebook, www.facebook.com/notes/facebook/ explaining-facebooks-spam-prevention-systems/403200567130/.
6. Statista recorded Google's lowest-ever market share of web searches—a staggering 86 percent—in the summer of 2018: www.statista.com/statistics/216573/worldwide -market-share-of-search-engines/.

7. Hay Kranen, "Linked Data and the Semantic Web: GLAM's Betting on the Wrong Horse?" Haykranen.nl, last modified May 19, 2014, www.haykranen.nl/2014/05/19/linked-data-and-the-semantic-web-glams-betting-on-the-wrong-horse/.

8. Tim Berners-Lee, "Linked Data: Design Issues," World Wide Web Consortium, last modified June 18, 2009, www.w3.org/DesignIssues/LinkedData.html.

9. *Wikipedia*, "Wikipedia: Statistics," https://en.wikipedia.org/wiki/Wikipedia:Statistics.

10. *Wikipedia*, "Help:Infobox," last modified October 17, 2018, https://en.wikipedia.org/wiki/Help:Infobox.

11. The Linked Open Data Cloud, https://lod-cloud.net/dataset/dbpedia.

12. Wikidata, "Wikidata: Notability," last modified July 1, 2019, www.wikidata.org/wiki/Wikidata:Notability.

13. That's 27,194,078 items without links, out of 53,147,530 total items in Wikidata as of December 2018: Wikimedia Foundation, https://tools.wmflabs.org/wikidata-todo/stats.php.

14. Open Data Institute, "First ODI Open Data Awards Presented by Sirs Tim Berners-Lee and Nigel Shadbolt," last modified November 4, 2014, https://oldsite.theodi.org/news/first-odi-open-data-awards-presented-by-sir-tim-berners-lee-and-sir-nigel-shadbolt.

15. "When we publicly launched Freebase back in 2007, we thought of it as a 'Wikipedia for structured data'": Google, last modified December 16, 2014, archived from the original at https://web.archive.org/web/20190206213838/https://plus.google.com/109936836907132434202/posts/bu3z2wVqcQc.

16. Thomas Pellissier Tanon, Denny Vrandečić, Sebastian Schaffert, Thomas Steiner, and Lydia Pintscher, "From Freebase to Wikidata: The Great Migration," *Proceedings of the 25th International Conference on World Wide Web* (2016): 1419–28, available at https://dl.acm.org/citation.cfm?id=2874809.

TEAR THE ROOF
OFF THE SUCKER
Linked Library Data

inked data services, applications, and tools have matured considerably since the early, exploratory years in Semantic Web research and development. As these technologies—along with business products and services—continue to be integrated into the daily lives of consumers, libraries and supporting information services have also found opportunities to augment the web with high-quality bibliographic and authority data. This opportunity has sparked library participation in Semantic Web conversations in a number of ways, including growing library linked-data programs and services in depth and scope and scaling collaboration efforts among participants. By publishing bibliographic information as linked data and connecting concepts to external datasets across domains, the library community has become an active participant in the rich linked information landscape; this participation is dynamic, complex, and ever-evolving. This particular chapter takes a brief look at how linked data has infiltrated, and subsequently taken shape, within the library community.

LIBRARY OF CONGRESS AUTHORITIES AS LINKED DATA

The bulk of the Library of Congress's efforts in bringing linked data to the library world is tracked in Angela Kroeger's article "The Road to BIBFRAME: The Evolution of the Idea of Bibliographic Transition into a Post-MARC Future." In it, Kroeger details a 2006 report commissioned by the LC, entitled "The Changing Nature of the Catalog and Its Integration with Other Discovery Tools," which investigated the perceived needs for future bibliographic description within the library community.[1] Though the released report predated the development of the term *linked data* by several months, it nevertheless found respondents envisioning "linked pools of data" for resource-searching, "rather than one data store for every kind of information object."[2] Another LC-affiliated report, "On the Record: Report of the Library of Congress Working Group on the Future of Bibliographic Control" (2008), acknowledged that the overall "bibliographic universe" was much bigger than just libraries, publishers, and organizations like the LC and OCLC, implying the time was nigh for building MARC's replacement.[3]

In between these two reports, the Library of Congress began investigating the use of linked data methods to bring its existing library-curated controlled vocabularies to the Semantic Web. In 2009, the LC released its Library of Congress Subject Headings (LCSH) as linked data, followed shortly thereafter by name authorities, genres, and other controlled lists of terms found in library data, through the LC Linked Data Service (LDS) at `http://id.loc.gov`. The LDS establishes stable URIs for name and subject authorities while also mapping them to semantic ontologies of the library world—predominantly, MADS/RDF and SKOS. As we mentioned in our chapter on ontologies, SKOS (Simple Knowledge Organization System) is a W3C standard originally designed by Ed Summers for representing thesauri, taxonomies, classification schemes, and subject heading lists as linked data. SKOS was designed as a broad solution to bring organization systems to the Semantic Web. MADS/RDF, on the other hand, is an RDF-mapped version of the Metadata Authority Description Schema (MADS), which was designed specifically to support library authority data; in fact, the MADS/RDF ontology is fully mapped to SKOS, allowing MADS/RDF to be used for more detailed triple statements than SKOS.

Using both of these ontologies, LDS aimed to make its thesauri amenable to just about any kind of linked-data consumer. Figure 6.1 diagrams a selection of the triples derived from the LC's original authority record describing

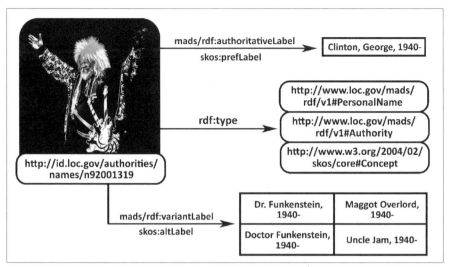

FIGURE 6.1
George Clinton authority record as RDF

George Clinton.[4] For reference, Clinton's authority record contains the following MARC data:

100 1_ $a Clinton, George, $d 1940-

400 0_ $a Dr. Funkenstein, $d 1940-

400 0_ $a Doctor Funkenstein, $d 1940-

400 0_ $a Maggot Overlord, $d 1940-

400 0_ $a Uncle Jam, $d 1940-

Our linked LC node maps the data found in the 100 (Main Personal Name Heading) MARC field to comparable properties in MADS/RDF (author-itativeLabel) and SKOS (prefLabel), just as the variant and esoteric names with which Clinton has been credited, found in 400 fields, are directed to skos:altLabel and mads/rdf:variantLabel properties. Finally, the Clinton node is described with an rdf:type property linked to major class types within the ontologies: PersonalName and Authority from MADS, and Concept from SKOS.

With its vocabularies brought into the linked data fold, it only made sense for the Library of Congress to begin rethinking the nature of bibliographic description and, ultimately, move forward on creating a replacement for MARC.

In November 2012 the LC released a primer on its Bibliographic Framework Initiative, or BIBFRAME, which was followed shortly afterward by a corresponding ontology in early 2013.

BIBFRAME
(You Knew We'd Have to Cover This)

BIBFRAME represents something of a quandary for this book. At the time of writing, BIBFRAME has been under development for close to a decade, and while some institutions are actively using it to experiment with data storage and cataloging, this would-be bibliographic standard is still conspicuously absent from the greater library life. At this point, there's enough history and information to write a small book on the BIBFRAME project alone, though a book about an as-yet unreleased data model would be comically vulnerable to a death of obsolescence. We run the same risk here; accordingly, this section will only wade into the shallower waters of BIBFRAME, discussing its foundational concepts and latest data model.

At its core, BIBFRAME is an upper-level linked data ontology that uniquely identifies real-world entities and concepts found in bibliographic data and exposes the relationships within that data through RDF. Though it was first announced in 2012, the roots of BIBFRAME go back to 1998, the year the International Federation of Library Associations and Institutions (IFLA) released its Functional Requirements for Bibliographic Records (FRBR), a conceptual model for bibliographic information retrieval in library catalogs and databases. FRBR proposed a restructuring of library catalog data, moving away from MARC's "flat" format—that is, a format that does not recognize or make explicit relationships between records—toward an entity-relationship (ER) model. A basic ER model explicitly indicates relationships that can exist between entities, or things of interest. (Sounds a bit like linked data, doesn't it?) FRBR presented a new conceptual bibliographic model that acknowledged the connectedness between information resources, while also stripping intellectual content from physical embodiments. The model consisted of three separate groups of entities:

1. Group 1 entities represent the by-products of some kind of intellectual or artistic expression, be it a written book, performed music, film, or some other kind of endeavor: *Work, Expression, Manifestation,* and *Item* (or WEMI);

2. Group 2 entities are the people and organizations responsible for the custodianship of Group 1's intellectual/artistic endeavors; and

3. Group 3 entities are the concepts, events, and places reflected in the intellectual/artistic endeavors.[5]

Much of the discussion around FRBR has focused on the modeling of Group 1 entities. While Groups 2 and 3 resembled the familiar name and subject authorities of library catalog data, respectively, Group 1 was completely new territory for librarians who were used to representing library materials through the 2nd edition of the *Anglo-American Cataloguing Rules* (AACR2) and MARC cataloging. We can illustrate the WEMI entities using our old friend, *Mothership Connection*, as a point of reference. *Work* represents the specific intellectual or artistic creation underlying the resource; as such, the *Work* concept is often an abstract idea, usually made physical or tangible through an *Expression*. In our case, *Work* is the collection of songs conceptually devised by members of Parliament, while *Expression* represents the musical recordings of those songs, sequenced together as a full-length album called *Mothership Connection*. *Manifestation* is some kind of physical embodiment of the *Expression*, with *Item* representing a single copy of that *Manifestation*; because libraries have traditionally collected and circulated mass-produced books, CDs, and movies, *Item* and *Manifestation* data tends to be what already exists in library catalog data. Previously, we noted that the Library of Congress's catalog carries two separate versions of *Mothership Connection*: an original vinyl pressing as well as a reissued CD version. These become two separate *Manifestations* of the same *Expression*, and the two actual copies held by the LC become *Items* of those respective *Manifestations*. The entities of Groups 2 and 3 augment and enrich the relationships of Group 1; much like the linked model that would appear just a handful of years later, these entities also facilitate connections to other resources. *Works* could have many different *Expressions* or *Manifestations*; *Works* could be about other *Works*; different resources can all point back to the same Group 2 author; and so on.

Though thought-provoking, FRBR was not without its critics. Librarian Karen Coyle pointed out that although FRBR did not explicitly advocate its use with any particular data structure, it was obvious that MARC was not adequate to express the model.[6] Nevertheless, in 2012, Resource Description and Access (RDA)—a bibliographic cataloging standard based on FRBR, along with the entity-relationship model—replaced AACR2 as the descriptive conventions for library cataloging. RDA was a necessary step forward for the development of bibliographic data, but its steering committee took great pains to remind the library community of its status as a content standard, not a storage or display format (like MARC). This left libraries with the task of having to hammer MARC into a shape that would accommodate the FRBR underpinnings of RDA.

BIBFRAME, on the other hand, is completely separate from the MARC format. As such, its data model adheres (fairly) closely to FRBR's entity-group design, with relationship connections made via RDF triples. The current edition of LC's BIBFRAME model—version 2.0, introduced in 2016—contains three core classes: *Work*, *Instance*, and *Item*.[7] *Work* and *Item* have carried over from their FRBR counterparts, while *Instance* is an amalgam of *Expression* and *Manifestation*, somewhat simplifying FRBR's design. FRBR's Group 2 and 3 entities have also been condensed into a handful of classes: *Agents* (people or organizations connected to a *Work* or *Instance*, such as musical groups like Parliament), *Subjects* (which are connected to *Work* nodes), and *Events*.[8] It should be noted, however, that the BIBFRAME 2.0 ontology goes beyond FRBR, holding almost 200 classes and over 100 properties associated with bibliographic description.[9] Using this ontology (along with actual BIBFRAME data created by the LC), we can adapt our *Mothership Connection* FRBR example into a diagram of linked data triples (see figure 6.2). Note that as an example of the *Work* class, *Mothership Connection* is disconnected from any of its physical forms; that domain is left to its *Instance* node—here, the specific instance is the vinyl album version from LCCN 00717929, the catalog record investigated in chapter 2. A handful of catalogers out there might ask: "But where's the catalog record?" Sure, the *Item* node attached to this *Work*/*Instance* data constitutes some of what catalogers might consider "traditional" library catalog data—for example, the *Item*'s rdfs:label is the call number attached to the LCCN 00717929 catalog record—but for all intents and purposes, these triples *are* a catalog record. The flat MARC record seen earlier has been dissected into three distinct parts: a high-level description of a musical album, a description of a particular physical version of that album, and a real-world copy of that physical version, held by a library. Each of these has its own unique URI, which means that adding extra copies of this particular vinyl album locally means adding new *Item* nodes; new editions—say, a remastered CD version of *Mothership Connection*—mean new *Instance* nodes connected to the *Work* node.

It should be noted that BIBFRAME 2.0 is not the only BIBFRAME ontology currently in existence. Back when the Library of Congress announced the BIBFRAME initiative, they contracted with Zepheira, a data management

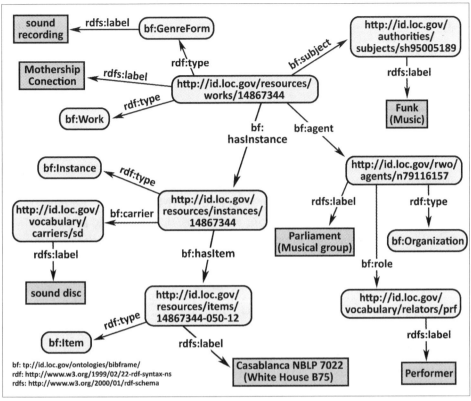

FIGURE 6.2

Mothership Connection **FRBR example as linked data**

company, to bring the project to fruition. The product of that partnership was the initial BIBFRAME data model, now referred to as BIBFRAME 1.0, released around 2012. Sometime between 2015 and 2016, the Library of Congress and Zepheira parted ways, splitting development into separate roads; the LC announced BIBFRAME 2.0, while Zepheira released an alternate ontology, BIBFRAME Lite. BIBFRAME Lite is based on version 1.0 of the data model. BIBFRAME 1.0—and thus BIBFRAME Lite—consist of four classes: *Work, Instance, Authority,* and *Annotation.*[10] Among a number of differences between the two models, version 1.0 uses an *Authority* class for people, places, and things; similarly, 1.0 uses the *Annotation* class to represent local holdings and item data. Additionally, BIBFRAME Lite employs a modular approach to bibliographic description; users can opt to employ one or more different "profiles," or curated components of BIBFRAME Lite's classes and properties. For example, the Lite vocabulary offers the "basic scaffolding" of bibliographic description (*Work,*

Instance, Authority, and *Annotation,* plus 24 other classes and 71 properties).[11] This can be expanded with one or more additional vocabularies—books and continuing resources, archival materials, rare materials, and early printing—or with all of them together in a "kitchen-sink" approach.[12]

SCHEMA.ORG'S BIB EXTENSION

In our last chapter, we touched on the existence of Schema.org, a linked data ontology used by many web search engines to process structured data on the internet. In mid-2012, OCLC announced they would be working with the Schema.org community, along with BIBFRAME cocreator Zepheira, to develop library-specific Schema.org extensions, describing the project as "a valuable two-way bridge between the library community and the consumer Web."[13]

Released in 2015, the bibliographic extension of Schema.org—referred to as Schema Bib Extend—added a number of class types commonly found in library catalogs: *Atlas, Audiobook, Chapter, Collection, Newspaper,* and *Thesis,* along with extensive properties for describing comic books and graphic novels.[14] Data using this extension, coupled with the standard Schema.org ontology, has been incorporated into OCLC's WorldCat, and is also part of Zepheira's Library .link partnership that brings BIBFRAME data to commercial library products from SirsiDynix iii Innovative. However, Schema Bib Extend also offers libraries a (relatively) low-barrier method of utilizing linked data: embedding linked, structured data within their OPACs and library home pages in order to gain greater visibility through search engine optimization (SEO). Numerous libraries of varying sizes have already undertaken similar projects to leverage their online standing with Google, Bing, and the like.[15]

DEEP DIVE
Schema-ing OPAC Data

Scenario: You want to try your hand at coding some items in your catalog with Schema.org-flavored linked data. How would you go about this? Like a lot of programmatic work, it helps to break the task down into separate subtasks. Let's go through each of the subtasks needed to take a library item—like a copy of *Mothership Connection*—and turn it into Schema.org linked data.

SUBTASK 1: Describe a CD copy of *Mothership Connection.* Let's use some of our previously established triple data to fill out a bare-bones JSON-LD object with Schema classes and properties, based on the sample triples we created in previous chapters:

```
<script type="application/ld+json">
  {
          "@context": "http://schema.org",
          "@type": "MusicAlbum",
          "@id": "https://our.library.fake/opac//0000001
#record",
          "name": "Mothership Connection",
          "genre": "funk",
          "sameAs": "http://tuneeggheadz.fake/byz6wd",
          "byArtist": {
                  "@type": "MusicGroup",
                  "name": "Parliament",
                  "@id": "http://our-db.fake/entity006"
          },
          "albumRelease": {
                  "@type": "MusicRelease",
                  "name": "Mothership Connection",
                  "@id": "http://our-db.fake/entity000"
          },
          "version": "CD"
  }
</script>
```

Here, we've taken the link to our (fake) OPAC record and turned it into a hash URI, so that we can identify our data object separately from the OPAC web page itself. (If you don't remember what a hash URI is, see chapter 5.)

SUBTASK 2: Use Schema.org to show that this real-world item is available from the library. Schema.org uses an additional class type, *Product*, to denote an object that can be acquired. Once a product is identified as an object's *additionalType* property, an *Offer* object is added to show how and where the object can be acquired:

```
"additionalType": "Product",
"offers":{
            "@type": "Offer",
            "availability": "http://schema.org/InStock",
            "serialNumber": "[item barcode]",
            "sku": "[item call number]",
            "businessFunction": "http://purl.org/good
relations/v1#LeaseOut",
            "availableAtOrFrom": "Circulation",
            "price": 0
    }
```

Adding *Product* metadata shows us that much of Schema.org's ontology is primarily built to foster commerce; as such, this means marking up our library item as if it were a product in a store with serial numbers (item barcodes), SKUs (item call number), and denoting that the offer is for "Lease" (using *LeaseOut* from the GoodRelations ontology) at a price of zero dollars.

SUBTASK 3: Identify the library as the entity offering the product. Finally, we can start adding structured, linked data about our library:

```
"offeredBy": {
      "@type": "Library",
      "@id": "http://library.anytown.gov#id",
      "name": "Anytown City Library",
      "url": "http://library.anytown.gov",
      "telephone": "555-555-5555",
      "address": "123 Quasar Lane, Anytown, State"
  }
```

Taken all together, we have created the following JSON-LD object, which can be embedded within the OPAC web page for this particular item, which can then be consumed by web crawlers:

```
<script type="application/ld+json">
{
        "@context": "http://schema.org",
        "@type": "MusicAlbum",
        "@id": "https://our.library.fake/opac//0000001
#record",
        "name": "Mothership Connection",
        "genre": "funk",
        "sameAs": "http://tuneeggheadz.fake/byz6wd",
        "byArtist":{
                "@type": "MusicGroup",
                "name": "Parliament",
                "@id": "http://our-db.fake/entity006"
        },
        "albumRelease":{
                "@type": "MusicRelease",
                "name": "Mothership Connection",
                "@id": "http://our-db.fake/entity000"
        },
        "version": "CD",
        "additionalType": "Product",
        "offers":{
                "@type": "Offer",
                "availability": "http://schema.org/InStock",
                "serialNumber": "[item barcode]",
                "sku": "[item call number]",
                "businessFunction": "http://purl.org/
goodrelations/v1#LeaseOut",
                "availableAtOrFrom": "Circulation",
                "price":0,
                "offeredBy":{
                        "@type": "Library",
                        "@id": "http://library.anytown.gov#id",
                        "name": "Anytown City Library",
                        "url": "http://library.anytown.gov",
                        "telephone": "555-555-5555",
                        "address": "123 Quasar Lane, Anytown,
State"
                }
        }
}
</script>
```

OTHER LINKED LIBRARY PROJECTS

Considering how early librarians and library-aligned organizations jumped on the linked data bandwagon, it's impossible to list every single linked library data project or ontology here. However, we will close this chapter out with a few short descriptions of notable and important linked-data projects that are involved with, or associated with, library data.

Virtual International Authority File

The Virtual Internet Authority File (VIAF) is a joint project linking several national library authority databases. Created in 2003 by the Library of Congress, the German National Library, and OCLC, VIAF is now a service operated by OCLC, combining the headings of more than seventy national libraries from around the world into unique, disambiguated names, works, and expressions. VIAF records are identified by URIs, and its data is downloadable as RDF at https://viaf.org/viaf/data/. Raw RDF/XML triples describing Parliament, for example, can be viewed by accessing https://viaf.org/viaf/148850890/rdf.

Medical Subject Headings

The Medical Subject Headings (MeSH) is a biomedical controlled vocabulary and thesaurus that is used for subject access to resources housed in the National Library of Medicine catalogs. It is available as a SPARQL endpoint (https://id.nlm.nih.gov/mesh/query), or is downloadable as N-Triples (ftp://ftp.nlm.nih.gov/online/mesh/rdf/mesh.nt.gz).

Art & Architecture Thesaurus

The Art & Architecture Thesaurus (AAT), managed and edited by the Getty Trust, is a cross-domain thesaurus intended to describe works of art, architecture, and archival materials. AAT was sparked by a desire for more consistent cataloging and information retrieval among art libraries, art journal indexing services, and museums. It is freely accessible for use as linked open data and is published under the Open Data Commons Attribution License (ODC-By) v1.0. A SPARQL endpoint and a variety of serializations are available for download at http://vocab.getty.edu.

Thesaurus of Geographic Names

Another Getty project, the Thesaurus of Geographic Names (TGN), is a subject list that describes places and physical features related to historical art and architecture. Like AAT, it is freely accessible for use as linked open data via its SPARQL endpoint (http://vocab.getty.edu/) or is downloadable as N-Triples (http://vocab.getty.edu/dataset/tgn/full.zip), and is published under the Open Data Commons Attribution License (ODC-By) v1.0.

Faceted Application of Subject Terminology

The Faceted Application of Subject Terminology (FAST), a subset of Library of Congress Subject Headings created by OCLC, is a controlled vocabulary aimed at being easily maintained, simple to browse, and universal enough for system interoperability. FAST emerged in the late 1990s at a time when OCLC was searching for a subject access system that could utilize Dublin Core-encoded records. FAST linked data is accessible in a number of ways, including via web browsers (http://experimental.worldcat.org/fast/), N-Triples (www.oclc.org/research/themes/data-science/fast/download.html), and via the FAST Linked Data API.

International Standard Name Identifier

The International Standard Name Identifier (ISNI) is a 16-digit identifier that uniquely identifies the identities of media creators and contributors. Created under the auspices of the International Organization for Standardization (ISO) and published as an ISO standard in 2012, ISNIs are governed and assigned by the ISNI International Authority (ISNI-IA), which includes OCLC as a founding member. ISNIs are built on linked data, with each ISNI accessible via URI; Parliament, for example, with 000000010944655X as its ISNI, can be found with the URI http://www.isni.org/isni/000000010944655X. ISNI records are available in both XML and human-readable HTML, and are freely available for querying and harvesting. As of 2019, libraries such as the British Library, Italy's Casalini Libri, Spain's Biblioteca Nacional de España, France's Bibliothèque Nationale de France, and the National Library of Korea are all registration agencies, providing an interface between ISNI applicants and their assignment.

LD4L and LD4P

Linked Data for Libraries (LD4L), a project awarded to Cornell University and funded between 2014 and 2016 through the Andrew W. Mellon Foundation, investigated how linked data and the Semantic Web could be harnessed for better end-user discoverability and access. This cross-institutional collaboration between Cornell, the Library Innovation Lab at Harvard University, and the Stanford University Libraries aimed to create a Semantic Web ecosystem that would harmonize bibliographic and archival descriptions with all data types generated by the operation, research, and teaching activities of the participant institutions. LD4L was followed by Linked Data for Production (LD4P), also funded by the Mellon Foundation, a study that saw Cornell, Harvard, and Stanford joined by Columbia University, Princeton University, and the Library of Congress to pilot the production of linked data for library materials between 2016 and 2018. The results of these studies can be viewed at www.ld4l.org/.

NOTES

1. Angela Kroeger, "The Road to BIBFRAME: The Evolution of the Idea of Bibliographic Transition into a Post-MARC Future," *Cataloging & Classification Quarterly* 51, no. 8 (2013): 873–90, https://doi.org/10.1080/01639374.2013.823584.
2. Karen Calhoun, "The Changing Nature of the Catalog and Its Integration with Other Discovery Tools," Final Report, Library of Congress, last modified March 17, 2006, 35–36.
3. Library of Congress, "On the Record: Report of the Library of Congress Working Group on the Future of Bibliographic Control," last modified January 9, 2008, www.loc .gov/bibliographic-future/news/lcwg-ontherecord-jan08-final.pdf.
4. Available at http://id.loc.gov/authorities/names/n92001319.html.
5. Barbara Tillett, "What Is FRBR? A Conceptual Model for the Bibliographic Universe," Library of Congress, originally published in *Technicalities* 25, no. 5 (2003), www.loc.gov/ cds/downloads/FRBR.PDF.
6. Karen Coyle, "Future Considerations: The Functional Library Systems Record," *Library Hi Tech* 22, no. 2 (2004): 166–74.
7. Library of Congress, "Overview of the BIBFRAME 2.0 Model (Bibliographic Framework Initiative)," last modified April 21, 2016, www.loc.gov/bibframe/docs/ bibframe2-model.html.
8. Library of Congress, "Overview of the BIBFRAME 2.0 Model."
9. A human-readable version of the Library of Congress's BIBFRAME ontology can be viewed at http://id.loc.gov/ontologies/bibframe.html.
10. Library of Congress, "Bibliographic Framework as a Web of Data: Linked Data Model and Supporting Services," last modified November 21, 2012, www.loc.gov/bibframe/ pdf/marcld-report-11-21-2012.pdf.

11. BIBFRAME Vocabulary, "BIBFRAME Lite," http://bibfra.me/view/lite/.

12. BIBFRAME Vocabulary, "BIBFRAME Lite," http://bibfra.me/view/library/; http://bibfra.me/view/archive/; http://bibfra.me/view/rare/; http://bibfra.me/view/aas/; http://bibfra.me/vocab/.

13. Bob Murphy, "OCLC Adds Linked Data to WorldCat.org," WorldCat, *News Releases* (blog), OCLC, last modified June 20, 2012, https://worldcat.org/arcviewer/7/OCC/2015/03/19/H1426803137790/viewer/file1303.html.

14. A human-readable version of the ontology can be viewed at https://bib.schema.org/.

15. A number of articles discuss different uses of Schema.org markup for library and cultural heritage collection materials: Dan Scott, "White Hat Search Engine Optimization (SEO): Structured Web Data for Libraries," *Partnership* 10, no. 1 (2015), https://journal.lib.uoguelph.ca/index.php/perj/article/view/3328; Jason Ronallo, "HTML5 Microdata and Schema.org," *Code4Lib Journal* no. 16 (February 3, 2012), http://journal.code4lib.org/articles/6400; Andreu Sulé, "Schema.org: An Enhanced Display of Search Engine Results and Much More," *BiD: Textos Universitaris de Biblioteconomia i Documentació* no. 34 (June 2015), http://bid.ub.edu/en/34/sule.htm; and Richard Wallis, Antoine Isaac, Valentine Charles, and Hugo Manguinhas, "Recommendations for the Application of Schema.org to Aggregated Cultural Heritage Metadata to Increase Relevance and Visibility to Search Engines: The Case of Europeana," *Code4Lib Journal* no. 36 (April 20, 2017), http://journal.code4lib.org/articles/12330.

FREAKY AND HABIT-FORMING

Linked Data Projects That Even Librarians Can Mess Around With

Most of this book has been spent introducing linked data and breaking down its concepts, but now it's time to start thinking about how linked data might be introduced into your individual work. Journal articles, grants, and conference presentations abound on linked library data, but many of these projects are so complex, resource-intensive, or highly technical that it's no wonder many librarians leave conference sessions in a daze, feeling like linked data is out of reach (or worse, irrelevant). But don't worry—there are plenty of avenues to dip your toe in the linked data pool without extensive training or technical chops. This chapter presents a variety of linked library data projects across a spectrum of functions, technical expertise, and resources, providing points of entry for those librarians who are curious about the topic.

PRE-PROJECT PREP

Solo or Group?

Linked data projects are a good way to apply theoretical concepts in practice using local data, and they can be an opportunity to lead change in organizations and build stronger collaborations across functional areas. A quick review of the largest projects in the linked open data community for libraries, archives, and museums reveals that the most successful of these are *not* one-person operations. To realize the goals of these projects, a team is required; and you should rest assured that even with a team in place, it is not necessary to have answers to every question. In fact, a fun aspect of these projects can be embracing the many unanswered questions, knowing that there is room to contribute directly to a community working on those answers . . . and asking new questions!

Teams can be formed in a variety of ways. Some organizations form a team representing different functional areas, or gather a group comprised of folks who already have a strong understanding of traditional cataloging duties. Some teams form around their shared responsibilities in working with data and then expand to include broader perspectives representing users. Because there are components of linked data that touch so many areas, the team members' interest is much more important than their specific skills or experience. In general, linked data projects may be of most interest to technical services and systems and technology roles, but archives and special collections have a real opportunity to benefit from this work by improving the discovery of their materials. And please don't forget about public services librarians or folks who work directly with users. There are often faculty or government entities that have excellent data competencies and use cases, and these folks can be interesting collaborative partners. Many projects will call upon disciplinary expertise to enhance data, and the linked data user experience is an area that is virtually unexplored. If you are at a smallish institution or want to include the perspective of specialists who may not be with your organization, consider teaming up with other local GLAM professionals, or starting a virtual team. There are opportunities for truly anyone working in any area of librarianship to contribute to the future of linked open data.

Once the potential team members have been identified, then the next step might be to start investigating the local landscape by starting some conversations about existing skill sets, identifying candidate datasets, and noting areas where additional capacity may need to be built. Linked data is often something library managers have heard about but are unsure how to address. Taking on a small-scale linked data project to investigate the readiness in your organization can be a valuable step toward securing larger-scale buy-in for larger linked data projects or for building a program.

ACTIVITY: Terms of the Trade

One of the first goals of the team should be to review linked data's foundational concepts and the terminology used in the linked data community. A good first topic for the group might be to go over any terms and concepts that seem unclear or need clarification through examples, such as:

- World Wide Web versus Semantic Web
- URIs versus URLs
- RDF statements versus records
- graphs, nodes, relationships
- triplestores
- controlled vocabularies versus ontology
- serialization
- SPARQL

Hopefully, this book can serve as a solid foundation for bringing these terms into effective usage for the team. (See the "Glossary" at the end of this book for definitions of many of the most important terms.) Linked data is no longer in its infancy, and these terms are a good primer for almost any librarian to master. Not everyone needs to know how to write a SPARQL query, but almost all of us should be conversant with the fact that *Wikipedia*—one of the most important research sources in the world and a website that most of us use every day—is backed behind the scenes by Wikidata, a structured knowledge base of linked data. Becoming conversant in the basic terminology and taking the time to familiarize others in our community with these concepts are great initial steps for engaging colleagues in the topic and spreading the linked data momentum to everyone in our profession.

Getting the Levels Right

We've already talked about the value of collaboration on a linked data project team, but let's look directly at the issue of limited IT resources. There are very few libraries that can claim they have *too much* IT support. (If you're in that situation, skip ahead!) If technology support is already competing with several other needs in your library, it can be difficult to contemplate asking for more time from technical support. True, IT support will be required to help implement linked data, but investigating a small-scale project is a great way to prepare for a (necessary) future conversation about resources. Much can be learned about common tools, potential workflows, and resources in the course of a thoughtful discussion on building a linked data program. Many of these tools are free or open-source, so experimentation can be undertaken easily, but having an enthusiastic application developer, systems administrator, web developer, or technology head in the room learning alongside the group can pay dividends later when you're moving from an experiment to something larger in scale. Thus, readers are highly encouraged to involve and engage IT folks early in the process of exploring the tools and technologies available for linked data work; even so, a linked data team can do a lot of legwork and set priorities *before* requesting support for a larger project.

LAYING THE FOUNDATION

Project 1

Inventorying Data in Your Library

TARGETED TO: Library Data Managers

Depending on the size or function of your library, your metadata may be held in a variety of locations and exist in a variety of formats. These are the "silos" so often mentioned in our community, and almost every division of the library has one: that Excel database of media collections; an Access database from a faculty member; catalog data; descriptive metadata for a digital collection of photographs; full-text digitized newspapers; paper inventories of an architectural drawings collection . . . All of these are possible linked open datasets of the future.

Another way to think of these assets is to pull in concepts from data science and think of them as "data lakes."[1] In a data lake, there might be various pipelines into the lake where data flows in or out, but the lake has boundaries and the data inside is not dynamically in motion. There is often a mix of data (or metadata), including structured and unstructured, cleaned and messy, in all formats and with a range of characteristics. This concept of data lakes is applied differently in data science, and mostly refers to digital data in a raw form, but it is useful to translate the concept into libraries.

We certainly have "pools" of metadata, usually in use with varying origin stories and qualities. Some metadata may come from commercial sources (electronic theses and dissertations), while other metadata might be created in-house (finding aids, digital objects). Still other forms of metadata are "messy" sets of data, such as homegrown databases, spreadsheets, and legacy collections. Finally, metadata may be hidden, or inaccessible in cases where there are unformatted inventories, files on old software versions, or even paper records. When considering a linked data project, ask yourself what data lakes exist, what silos of data are present in the organization, and what valuable information might be leveraged from an obsolete or more simplistic metadata format if it were structured and cleaned up. This kind of library data inventory is a good way to start documenting the characteristics of data that is available for a linked data project. An example project might look like this:

1. Identify and inventory data lakes of interest to the team. What library systems are in use and what types of content and data formats do they contain?

2. Compare the selected datasets to the 5-Star Linked Data model mentioned in chapter 5 and rate each of the sets. What would be needed to move each set to the next star-rating in the model? Is one set further along than the others?

3. After completing this inventory, identify a small dataset (or subset of the data) suitable for experimentation (somewhere between 100 and 200 records of detailed data that is currently publicly available).

4. Have the owner/data manager export the data out of the system and evaluate it by deciding on fields to keep, fields to delete, and fields that need to be added (enhanced) for the set to be effectively linked to other datasets. (If the data can't be exported . . . well, that's a good lesson learned!)

5. Try moving the data into a different software (for instance, from Excel into an open source data-cleaning program) or system (say, from an archival management system into a catalog, or between two digital repositories). Note the differences in the level of description, the system field requirements, and review any documented descriptive practices and how they might differ. Make notes about these and talk with a

metadata librarian about mapping and application profiles in order to understand their role in data creation and management.

6. Note any datasets that are available for public download and the format of the data. How is it prepared for consumption?

7. Note if any controlled vocabularies that have assigned URIs are being used within the data; if not, might a local vocabulary or ontology be of use?

Congratulations: You have just significantly upped your understanding of your local data and its transferability. That's a great first step to understanding the benefits and challenges of working with linked data. Don't get discouraged if your exploration reveals many less-than-perfect datasets; metadata folks will tell you that data quality is a huge and never-ending component of their work. You don't have to "clean" every dataset in order to do linked data work but beware of any project proposed that assumes automated data migration or that oversimplifies data transfer. Moreover, there is a reason why librarian job descriptions are trending toward data management qualifications, and this small project can be a great place to start identifying professional development opportunities that data managers across the library may need in order to ramp up capacity in working with data.

Project 2

Tools and Basic Technologies

TARGETED TO: Library Data Managers, Data Instructors, and Service Providers

Speaking of professional development, this follow-up activity digs deeper into exploring specific tools and technologies that are commonly used in linked data work. A good place to start is within the team, discussing the tools each functional area uses, and teaching and training each other on tools that are already in use or are available at no additional cost. Identifying these tools and deciding on "homework" or experiments with them completes the project goal of building the confidence and functional expertise of the team.

There will probably be a great deal of experience with *Microsoft Excel* across the organization; it can be interesting to start from the standpoint of focusing on the variety of functions and expertise that are applied in the daily use of spreadsheets. A whole session could be devoted to spreadsheet flavors, variations, and varieties across the library. This may also be a good time to discuss the organization's use of Google Sheets and how they vary from Excel.

Another common data cleanup tool is *OpenRefine*, formerly known as Google Refine. On the surface, this open-source tool looks like a spreadsheet but under the hood, it contains many of the powerful data transformation tools found in popular programming languages. OpenRefine can import and export a wide variety of data formats, and with extensions, it can not only produce RDF triples in a variety of serializations, but also interact with information from Wikidata. If the team does not have an OpenRefine user in the group, don't fret—a variety of free OpenRefine video tutorials exist, including ones produced by the site Programming Historian.[2]

A final area of technology tool experimentation deals with the management of vocabularies and their URIs. The team may want to review where vocabulary management is happening in their organization and refer back to any metadata application profiles in use. Are URIs being captured for these vocabularies? Is there a place to capture them if they aren't currently being captured? What about any local terms? Controlled vocabularies are a rich source of links for data, and it is worth looking into their management. Some organizations may manage terms in spreadsheets, Excel look-up tables, repository vocabulary modules, or outside tools such as Omeka or TemaTres.[3] The Western Name Authority Project offers some detailed information about managing local terms for linked open data.[4]

EXPERIMENTING WITH LINKED DATA CONCEPTS

The Star of the Show: Metadata Managers

Linked-data project teams with a good handle on important concepts and a familiarity with local data may be ready to jump into the exciting process of transforming data. This is often the step that makes clear just how the high-level linked data principles translate into specific changes in practice when looking at our data. In this section, we will lean heavily on our team's metadata managers to understand more about the work they typically lead; the goal is to practice getting outside the catalog-record mindset and inside the triple format. Specifically, we will discuss

- designing larger-scale metadata remediation and enhancement activities;

- how to identify candidate projects and manage the work; and
- exploring the details of how we manifest linked data from good, clean metadata.

Project 3

Adjusting the Levels:
Remediating and Enhancing Metadata

TARGETED TO: Library Data Managers,
Catalogers, and Metadata Creators

Many librarians have been in the situation of receiving a "collection" of electronic records or some other package of miscellaneous data; our background makes us the most logical endpoint to provide order out of this chaos. The explosion of digitized materials, electronic publishing, research data, and born-digital archival collections means that we are beginning to do this on a large scale, especially when confronted with greatly increased demand from users. There are now efforts underway to cope with this explosion. The prevalence of philosophies that encourage ramping up our efficiency and the use of "good enough" data is reflected in journal articles like "More Product, Less Process" and the practices that have emerged out of this trend.[5] Certainly, metadata librarians are threading the needle on balancing accuracy and richness of data with resource expenditure and time. This refrain—to let go of perfection and become comfortable with minimal processing for greater access—is a common one, and it presents interesting challenges for the world of linked open data. While we can't address this interesting debate here, we can highlight the fact that perhaps an approach to minimal processing for linked open data could acknowledge the need to invest in data quality but respect the scale at which data is being published. Maybe instead of "more product, less process," we should say "invest less, but invest smarter."

Smart investment in data remediation projects requires an understanding of where you will get the best return on that investment. It also requires attention to the nuances of the collection and an awareness of the way that linked open data may be consumed. The following activities address three key areas where value can be added to data through strategic investments.

ACTIVITY: Evolve Your Metadata Application Profile (MAP)

Application profiles are sets of metadata elements, policies, and guidelines defined for a particular application. Here is another place where your friendly metadata expert can work with your linked data team to educate and assess the current metadata application profile(s) in use at your organization.

1. Identify any MAPs in use and the last date of revision. Don't have any MAPs? The team may want to participate in creating one!

2. Perhaps the profile needs a refresh to currently used elements, vocabularies, or practices. A good exercise can be to conduct a field-by-field comparison with another trusted MAP from a larger organization or a more diverse set of collections and review which fields are missing, where the two profiles differ, and discuss why. The group, working with the metadata librarian, can submit recommendations for a revision, as well as some communication methods for sharing the new profile out to its users.

3. Audit a data collection while looking at the current or revised MAP and give your metadata a grade. Is the metadata in compliance? What types of problems exist? Sort the problems into small-scale fixes, medium-sized projects, and major resource investments in a report that can be used to prioritize remediation projects.

ACTIVITY: Audit Vocabularies and Add Identifiers

Get your data linked-ready! This means figuring out if your metadata creators are using controlled vocabularies accurately, finding vocabularies that have URIs, and creating a plan of action to start capturing them. There may also be an identified need to go back to legacy collections in order to match up your metadata with external ontologies and controlled vocabularies. This process is called *reconciliation*, and the result is the addition of URIs to your data. One of OpenRefine's most powerful features is reconciling data to external vocabularies. While OpenRefine cannot currently reconcile against SPARQL endpoints, several OpenRefine reconciliation services exist for linked datasets, most notably Wikidata. This means that if your data includes names, places, and other examples of individual nodes, you can try to match your data to the nodes in Wikidata; if you find any matches, you can then extract their URIs to add to your data. Note that simply adding URIs to your data does not automatically make it semantic or linked data; you are, however, taking a significant step forward by adding information that will aid in moving your data to a future linked-data environment. (You will find countless videos explaining and demoing OpenRefine's Reconciliation feature online.)

But what if your data is MARC? Luckily, the MARC format has a defined and controlled area for capturing URIs representing controlled authorities in records: the subfield zero ($0). Our example *Mothership Connection* MARC record from chapter 2 identifies Parliament, using a Library of Congress Name Authority heading, as the album's primary creator in the 110 (Main Entry -- Corporate Name) field:

```
110 2_ $a Parliament (Musical group)
```

The corresponding LC Name Authority heading is defined at the URI http://id.loc.gov/authorities/names/n79116157. Our field using this URI would look like this:

```
110 2_ $a Parliament (Musical group) $0 http://id.loc
.gov/ authorities/names/n79116157
```

The MARC format also identifies the subfield one ($1) as a controlled area to describe what it refers to as "Real World Object URIs"—which, for our purposes, means linked-data URIs representing a person, place, or other node, rather than a heading in LC's name and subject controlled vocabularies. Parliament is defined in the Virtual Internet Authority File (VIAF) with the URI http://viaf.org/viaf/148850890. We can now append our 110 field as:

```
110 2_ $a Parliament (Musical group) $0 http://id.loc
.gov/ authorities/names/n79116157 $1 http://viaf.org/
viaf/148850890
```

(You may be asking: What's the difference between an LC name heading URI and a VIAF URI that represents a conglomeration of authority headings? The answer is, functionally, there isn't a difference. The use of two different subfields comes down to the fact that the subfield zero was originally defined as a place to record the system control number of related authority records; it was redefined later on to include URIs, but it still retains the ability to store non-URI control numbers, which is likely why subfield one was subsequently created to store non-authority URIs.[6] Oh, silly MARC!)

This works fine when we're adding one or two URIs to a record. But adding URIs to hundreds of thousands of records, if not millions, requires programmatic approaches. Fortunately, the MarcEdit app features a "Link Identifier" tool in its "MARCNext" section; simply enter a source file of MARC records, choose which controlled vocabularies to search, and let it process. That being said, there are plenty of other ways to automate such a reconciliation task; you should work with your metadata librarian to find them. Again, the resulting MARC is not RDF, but the more your data links out to controlled authorities, the better "linked" your data can be in the future.

Project 4

Laying Down Some Tracks:
The Basics of Graphs and RDF

TARGETED TO: Metadata Managers, Subject Experts,
and Linked Data Team

One of the most interesting aspects of linked open data is its ability to open up a whole new way of browsing our datasets through the different ways their items may be related. This activity—much like our sample *Mothership Connection* diagrams in chapter 3—is intended to get your curators and subject experts involved, since they may see how they can contribute to linked open data by adding value. The following activity reveals this potential by getting your linked-data interest group together and graphing a complex web of relationships.

ACTIVITY: Diagram Triples and Graph Relationships

1. Find a suitable data "collection" with interesting relationships. This could be family history records, a journal article with multiple authors and institutions, an oral history collection, or a set of photographs capturing an event.
2. On paper (or a whiteboard), start listing out the subjects and what you can see about them from the physical objects in front of you.
3. Once you have a list, begin constructing triples by using natural language to describe the relationships (predicates) to other things (object nodes). Maybe one of your subject nodes has literal values that can be added? Remember, a subject in one case might turn out to be an object in another! Don't worry at this point about whether the predicates are "real" attributes from existing linked-data ontologies; just get comfortable with constructing the triples and playing with the linked data grammar.

4. Once you have a robust graph with lots of information, assign group members the homework of researching and assigning URIs to both subject/object nodes and predicates from real-life ontologies. When the group returns, collate the data in a single graph. This is a great way to see how relationships and rich metadata in the linked data world are limited only by the time and resources devoted to researching and creating the triples.

SHARING, SEEING, AND LINKING

As you may recall, linked open data only gets the highest rating in the 5-Star Data model if it is published and links out to other linked datasets. There is a lot to consider when talking about making your linked open data available to others as a dataset, such as time, cost of resources, and your ability to provide URIs that will exist indefinitely. These big-picture issues are good fodder for any linked-data interest group to discuss. Specific instructions for triplestores and data exchange protocols are a bit beyond the scope of this book, but it is important to think broadly about how to publish the data and what implications are associated with maintaining linked open data for others. The following exercises can be used to drive some of these conversations.

Project 5

Audience Participation:
Linked Data in Communities

TARGETED TO: Linked Data Team, Data Managers,
Subject Specialists, Archivists, and Digital Humanities Folks

ACTIVITY: Explore the Linked Data Landscape

Select a community you work with (archives, scholarly publishing, museums, humanities, newspapers, etc.) and identify a community-specific linked data project. Identify the status of the project and evaluate if you'd want to be involved in this community. What might you contribute, and what might your participation help you gain in terms of skills?

ACTIVITY: Evaluate Where to Engage in the Linked Data Community

Compile a list containing several linked data authorities (Library of Congress, Getty, Geonames, FAST, etc.) and several linked open data library projects. Divide these among the group members and have them visit the websites and audit them for the following items:

- Is the data accessible and loading quickly?
- Is there a "Date published"?
- Is there a "Data refreshed"?
- Is there an About section?
- Can the data be downloaded? Queried?
- Is there a contact person listed with an e-mail?
- Is there project documentation? Does the site look actively maintained?

Compare notes on the sites and discuss what is most important to the group in the evaluation. Use these notes to create a checklist for publishing linked open data at your library.

> Project 6

Real-World Data

TARGETED TO: Library Data Managers, Linked Data Team,
Catalogers, and Metadata Creators

So far, our linked data projects have been pretty much behind-the-scenes. And admittedly, a lot of linked data work is out of the spotlight and in the trenches of data work. This contributes to a bit of a messaging challenge when bringing up the topic with folks who may tolerate a certain amount of technical talk and metadata mumbling, but who really just want to get to the point: "What does it *look* like?" If folks can't see linked data, they probably won't think they should care much about it. Let's look at a few projects that help to increase familiarity with linked data and show the benefits of linked data in a research scenario.

ACTIVITY: Foolin' Around with Schema.org
on the Structured Data Testing Tool

Google provides a means to visualize structured, linked data embedded within web pages that use Schema.org markup. Called the Structured Data Testing

Tool (or SDTT, located at https://search.google.com/structured-data/test-ing-tool), it allows users to enter a URL or snippet of code, and Google will present the structured data found on that page/in that code exactly how Google's crawlers would see it. The SDTT will also alert you if it finds any errors in the structured data.

For this activity, compile a list of URLs to send through the SDTT; these can be regular websites you visit on a daily basis, as well as library and OPAC pages. Does the SDTT find any linked data on them? If it does, what happens when you change the code and rerun it?

Note that while Google has implemented quite a bit of Schema.org's ontology for recognizing structured, linked data, Google does not recognize all of it, especially some of the classes and properties found in expansion vocabularies (like the Bibliographic extension detailed in chapter 6). Try making your own JSON-LD objects for items in your library and run them through the SDTT. Does it recognize their `@type` classes? If not, how might this hinder the findability of library materials on a large-scale Schema.org embedding project?

ACTIVITY: SPARQLing

A number of linked datasets now offer SPARQL endpoints for public querying. One of these is the Wikidata Query Service (or WQS, located at https://query.wikidata.org/), which was covered in chapter 5. WQS offers over 400 examples of SPARQL queries used to generate comparative research based on the triples contained within Wikidata.

For this activity, investigate some of the example SPARQL queries available at the WQS; find one that seems interesting and run the example query. WQS will automatically generate a "Query Helper" panel so that you understand exactly what information is being requested. Once you click the big blue "play" button, the query will run and the output will be presented below.

Once you have run through some queries, try modifying some of them with new parameters and try to run them. What happens? What kind of information can you acquire by making your own SPARQL queries? For example, the "Biologists With Twitter Accounts" sample query returns over 500 Wikidata records of people who have the occupation of "Biologist" and a listed Twitter username. How many will you find if you change the occupation parameter to "Librarian"?

ASSESSING AND SUSTAINING

Project 7

Assessing Linked Data

TARGETED TO: Linked Data Team, Assessment Librarians,
Advocates for Users, and Library Managers

Despite our work in project 6, there just aren't that many places to go and "look at" linked open data. This is an acknowledged challenge and an area for future research in the field. Further exploration of the user experience could be an exciting, and much-needed, project that has the potential to help others working on assessing linked open data for users.

ACTIVITY: Review the Literature (Usability)

A small amount of literature exists on the user experience of linked open data. Seek out a few articles for the interest group to read, summarize, and discuss. Some possible starting points include the following resources:

Fagan, Jody Condit, Meris A. Mandernach, Carl S. Nelson, Jonathan R. Paulo, and Grover Saunders, "Usability Test Results for a Discovery Tool in an Academic Library," 2012, https://doi .org/10.6017/ital.v31i1.1855.

Hanrath, Scott, and Miloche Kottman, "Use and Usability of a Discovery Tool in an Academic Library," *Journal of Web Librarianship* 9, no. 1 (2015): 1–21, doi: 10.1080/19322909 .2014.983259.

Pekala, Shayna, "Microdata in the IR: A Low-Barrier Approach to Enhancing Discovery of Institutional Repository Materials in Google," *Code4Lib Journal,* no. 39 (2018), https://journal .code4lib.org/articles/13191.

Thakker, D., F. Yang-Turner, and D. Despotakis, "User Interaction with Linked Data: An Exploratory Search Approach," *International Journal of Distributed Systems and Technologies* 7, no. 1 (2016): 79–91, http://hdl.handle.net/10454/10874.

ACTIVITY: Review the Literature (Privacy and Use)

Linked data presents many use cases where there may be highly rich data that is linked to other datasets, creating relationships without any human intervention. How does this play out with personal or sensitive materials? If a digital object is offensive or created with malice yet widely shared, what responsibility do humans have to manage data that may take on a life of its own? What about privacy? The resources listed below focus on this aspect of linked data assessment and are sure to provoke a lively discussion:

* ScienceDirect, "Big and Open Linked Data (BOLD) in Government: A Challenge to Transparency and Privacy?," www.sciencedirect.com/science/article/pii/S0740624X15001069.
* Solid, https://solid.mit.edu/.
* World Wide Web Consortium, "Privacy," www.w3.org/Privacy/permissions-ws-2018/papers/axel-polleres.pdf.

Project 8

Make the Case for Linked Resources

TARGETED TO: Linked Data Team, Metadata Experts, and Library Managers

Let's look back on what you have explored in these hands-on linked data activities and projects. What have you learned and where do you want to focus energy now? Is there a particular local project that needs to be sustained? If so, great! Now it's time to keep the momentum going by sharing your newfound knowledge of linked data with the folks who control resources and who can help make your project happen in a larger way.

ACTIVITY: Pitching a Plan to the Administration

Gather your group and reflect on your research and hands-on experience with linked open data. Brainstorm ideas for a project and map out a plan. Write a proposal aimed at your library's administration to pursue a linked open data project on a larger scale. The plan might include the following sections:

* Introduction to Linked Data
* Goals of the Project

* How the Library Will Benefit
* Resource Needs
    * Staff Roles
    * Technology Needs
    * Funding
* Timeline for Project Completion
* Assessment Plan
* Post-Project Plan (i.e., how to sustain the project)
* Assessment Plan

Highlight the collaborative nature of the linked data study group or interest group team in order to show the value and the broader impact of continuing the work. Be ready to break down the concepts and do demonstrations in order to arouse interest and enthusiasm. Call on your metadata experts to hone their linked-data elevator speeches for the administration. Even if the project is not accepted immediately, this kind of planning can be a great start for a small grant proposal or a collaborative project with a partner who may be further along with linked open data. What is important is that now the idea exists! And now that linked data is no longer a blurry theoretical concept, but a reality—one that can be evolved, scaled, and customized to meet local resource availability and institutional need—how do we make it work for us?

NOTES

1. Bernard Marr, "What Is a Data Lake? A Super-Simple Explanation for Anyone," *Forbes*, last modified August 27, 2018, www.forbes.com/sites/bernardmarr/2018/08/27/what-is-a-data-lake-a-super-simple-explanation-for-anyone/.
2. *The Programming Historian*, https://programminghistorian.org.
3. TemaTres Controlled Vocabulary server, www.vocabularyserver.com.
4. Google, "Western Name Authority File Project," https://sites.google.com/site/westernnameauthorityfile/project-work-plan/vocabulary-software.
5. Mark A. Greene and Dennis Meissner, "More Product, Less Process: Revamping Traditional Archival Processing," *American Archivist* 68 (2005): 208–63.
6. Library of Congress, Network Development and MARC Standards Office, "Appendix A - Control Subfields," www.loc.gov/marc/bibliographic/ecbdcntf.html.

THE UNPROVABLE PUDDING
Where Is Linked Data in Everyday Library Life?

A t this point, you may be asking: "Okay, I know more about linked data, so what will I be expected to do? Where and when will this affect my work?"

To recap, linked data is a way of structuring data in order to leverage its relationships in a way that computers can more easily traverse, enabling different kinds of resource exploration and discovery. Existing library data holds vibrant information about our communal resources but is often locked up in an aging data format and structured in ways that make its contents less conducive to computer manipulation and processing. By moving beyond a format like MARC to semantic data models, we can make use of rich data created over many decades by library, archives, and museum workers.

In a personal sense, moving towards and "doing" linked data will look different to everyone. Some, inspired by the projects described in this book, will get to the next steps—learning more, engaging in linked data projects, perhaps even building their own triplestore. Some, similarly inspired by the projects described in this book, will engage by observing these projects unfold in their domain with a deeper understanding of the underlying technologies and their importance to the future of the GLAM community. Other readers may be satisfied with a fuller understanding of these technologies and will wait to see it materialize in their daily work. All of these are the right steps forward.

Unfortunately, we cannot say if this will be enough. At the beginning of this book, we told you that this text alone will not turn you into a linked data pro. The truth is, we're not even sure what a linked library data pro looks like right now. Is it someone who creates RDF data? Is it someone who can install and keep a triplestore up and running? Is it someone who has mastered the art of SPARQL?

Part of the reason we don't know is because despite the constant conference presentations and theoretical journal articles, libraries and librarians, by and large, don't "do" linked data. The results of the International Linked Data Survey for Implementers, conducted by OCLC in 2014 and 2018, underscored the need for education and experience around linked data in libraries. Both surveys found that even among project implementers, the biggest barrier to publishing linked data is the "steep learning curve for staff," which was cited nearly twice as much as "lack of resources" as a barrier.[1] But the problem is not just linked data's learning curve or the access to education itself; as we write this book, it is now almost ten years since the Library Congress announced the BIBFRAME project. Since then, a handful of institutions have published collections, either whole or in part, as BIBFRAME; meanwhile, the Ex Libris Alma and SirsiDynix BLUEcloud Visibility library service platforms can generate BIBFRAME data for the collections of their customers. But while MARC was never expected to permanently disappear from the library scene, the library community has in no way begun to phase it out of common use.

Taken together, this leaves the library community in a sort of limbo, knowing that we can't afford to continue using an obsolete format but also bereft of the tools needed to transition away from it. "If the proof of the pudding is in the eating," writes Ruth Kitchin Tillman, "I would argue that linked data is currently a pudding that [librarians] can smell—and most of the time it smells delicious—but it's always out of reach and never edible." She continues:

> How is it that we can learn to do things in HTML, XML, MARC, and even SQL while linked data is often an extra reach? I believe it's because of the systems that exist. We simply do not have the systems

to match our vision. Instead, we have what are essentially a bunch of databases working in triples. They can be very nice databases. They're very expansive because we can create new predicates. . . . When it comes to linked data that you or I can actually create, outside of [DBpedia or Wikidata]-type projects, we're often limited to embedding schema.org data in our websites. Hurrah for providing structured, machine-usable data. But we're still not fulfilling the dream or promise of linked data.[2]

Libraries are not alone in the failure to realize the potential of linked data; in fact, linked data practitioners acknowledge that the Semantic Web itself remains largely unrealized. Ruben Verborgh, a professor of Semantic Web technology at Ghent University in Belgium, notes that the evangelism of linked data rarely leverages the very technology being preached, due in no small part to the fact that the evangelists lack Semantic Web experience as both developers and users: "If we keep on finding excuses for not using our own research outcomes, how can we convince others?" He continues:

> Our fallacy has been our insistence that the remaining part of the road [to a Semantic Web] solely consisted of code to be written. We have been blind to the substantial research challenges we would surely face if we would only take our experiments out of our safe environments into the open Web. Turns out that the engineers and developers have moved on and created their own solutions, bypassing many of the lessons we have learned, because we stubbornly refused to acknowledge the amount of research needed to turn our theories into practice.[3]

All of this may seem bleak, but it is helpful to remember that the tide is turning, slow though it may be. Innovation and change require vision and perseverance, two qualities the GLAM community has proved capable of mastering time and time again. The tide will begin to turn faster when librarians leave the confines of their comfort zones and begin learning about new ways to achieve our community's age-old goals. Regardless of the technology, the vision is clear: improved and enhanced access to information and cultural heritage resources through cataloging and metadata practices.

However, only when we, as practitioners and researchers, are able to articulate our needs to create and use linked data, will we be able to work together to take full advantage of its potential. For some, this may include deep technical expertise, while for many others, a general understanding is sufficient to participate in the conversations. In either case, by furthering our collective understanding, expertise, and participation in linked data, the library community gets closer to tasting the proverbial pudding. While you're at it, why not get up from the table and join us in the kitchen? There's plenty of pudding to go around, and it's a lot more satisfying to make it together.

NOTES

1. OCLC, "Linked Data Survey," www.oclc.org/research/themes/data-science/linkeddata/linked-data-survey.html.
2. Ruth Kitchin Tillman, "Linked Data Is Made of Systems," Ruthtillman.com, last modified May 16, 2019, http://ruthtillman.com/linked-data-is-made-of-systems/.
3. Ruben Verborgh, "The Semantic Web Identity Crisis: In Search of the Trivialities That Never Were," Ruben.verborgh.org, last modified May 21, 2019, https://ruben.verborgh.org/articles/the-semantic-web-identity-crisis/.

BIBLIOGRAPHY

Anglo-American Cataloguing Rules. 2nd ed. Chicago: American Library Association, 1978.

Avram, Henriette D. *MARC: Its History and Implications.* Washington, DC: Library of Congress Development Office, 1975. https://files.eric.ed.gov/fulltext/ED127954.pdf.

Berners-Lee, Tim. "Axioms of Web Architecture." World Wide Web Consortium. Last modified August 27, 2009. www.w3.org/DesignIssues/Rules.html.

———. "A Brief History of the Web." World Wide Web Consortium. www.w3.org/DesignIssues/TimBook-old/History.html.

———. "Giant Global Graph." Decentralized Information Group, Massachusetts Institute of Technology. Last modified November 21, 2007. Archived from the original at https://web.archive.org/web/20160713021037/; http://dig.csail.mit.edu/breadcrumbs/node/215.

———. "Linked Data: Design Issues." World Wide Web Consortium. Last modified June 18, 2009. www.w3.org/DesignIssues/LinkedData.html.

———. "The Original Proposal of the WWW, HTMLized." World Wide Web Consortium. www.w3.org/History/1989/proposal.html.

———. "Semantic Web: Why RDF Is More Than XML." World Wide Web Consortium. Last modified October 14, 1998. www.w3.org/DesignIssues/RDF-XML.html.

———. *Weaving the Web.* San Francisco: Harper San Francisco, 1999.

———. "World Wide Web Servers." World Wide Web Consortium. www.w3.org/History/19921103-hypertext/hypertext/DataSources/WWW/Servers.html.

Berners-Lee, Tim R. Fielding, and L. Masinter. "Uniform Resource Identifier (URI): Generic Syntax." Network Working Group, IETF Tools. Last modified January 2005. https://tools.ietf.org/html/rfc3986.

Borst, Willem Nico. "Construction of Engineering Ontologies." PhD thesis, Institute for Telematica and Information Technology, University of Twente, Netherlands, 1997. https://ris.utwente.nl/ws/portalfiles/portal/6036651/t0000004.pdf.

Calhoun, Karen. "The Changing Nature of the Catalog and Its Integration with Other Discovery Tools, Final Report." Library of Congress, 2006. www.loc.gov/catdir/calhoun-report-final.pdf.

The Cernettes. "Cernettes: The Bios." https://cernettes.wixsite.com/cernettes/the-bios.

Columbus, Louis. "10 Charts That Will Change Your Perspective of Amazon Prime's Growth." *Forbes.* Last modified March 4, 2018. www.forbes.com/sites/louiscolumbus/2018/03/04/10-charts-that-will-change-your-perspective-of-amazon-primes-growth/.

Coyle, Karen. "Future Considerations: The Functional Library Systems Record." *Library Hi Tech* 22, no. 2 (2004): 166–74. https://doi.org/10.1108/07378830410524594.

Discogs. "Parliament -- Mothership Connection." www.discogs.com/Parliament-Mother ship-Connection/master/15841.

Dueber, Bill. "ISBN Parenthetical Notes: Bad MARC Data #1." Robot Librarian. Last modified April 2011. http://robotlibrarian.billdueber.com/2011/04/isbn-parenthetical -notes-bad-marc-data-1/.

Europeana. "Europeana Data Model Primer." Last modified July 14, 2013. https://pro .europeana.eu/files/Europeana_Professional/Share_your_data/Technical_requirements/ EDM_Documentation/EDM_Primer_130714.pdf.

Fensel, Dieter. *Ontologies: A Silver Bullet for Knowledge Management and Electronic Commerce.* London: Springer, 2004.

"The First Search Engine, Archie." Last modified September 21, 2002. Archived from the original at https://web.archive.org/web/20110719211803/; www.isrl.illinois.edu/~chip/ projects/timeline/1990archie.htm.

Gayo, Jose E. Labra, Eric Prud'hommeaux, Iovka Boneva, and Dimitris Kontokostas. *Validating RDF Data.* Synthesis Lectures on the Semantic Web: Theory and Technology 7, no. 1 (2018). https://doi.org/10.2200/S00786ED1V01Y201707WBE016.

Google, Freebase. "When we publicly launched Freebase back in 2007, we thought of it as a 'Wikipedia for structured data'. . ." Last modified December 16, 2014. Archived from the original at https://web.archive.org/web/20190206213838/; https://plus.google .com/109936836907132434202/posts/bu3z2wVqcQc.

Greene, Mark A., and Dennis Meissner. "More Product, Less Process: Revamping Traditional Archival Processing." *American Archivist* 68 (2005): 208–63. www.archivists .org/prof-education/pre-readings/IMPLP/AA68.2.MeissnerGreene.pdf.

Gruber, Thomas R. "Toward Principles for the Design of Ontologies Used for Knowledge Sharing?" *International Journal of Human-Computer Studies* 43, no. 5–6 (November 1995): 907–28. https://doi.org/10.1006/ijhc.1995.1081.

Holloway, Ruth. "3 Open Source Code Libraries to Handle MARC-Formatted Records." OpenSource.com. Last modified April 21, 2017. https://opensource.com/article/17/4/ bit-about-marc-handlers.

Hough, Andrew. "How the First Photo Was Posted on the Web 20 Years Ago." *Telegraph*, July 11, 2012. www.telegraph.co.uk/technology/news/9391110/How-the-first-photo -was-posted-on-the-Web-20-years-ago.html.

Indiewebcamp. "The Open Graph Protocol." Last modified April 30, 2019. https://indieweb .org/The-Open-Graph-protocol.

Internet Live Stats. "Total Number of Websites." Last modified August 2019. www.internet livestats.com/total-number-of-websites/.

Isaacson, Walter. *The Innovators.* New York: Simon & Schuster, 2014.

JSON.org. "JSON: The Fat-Free Alternative to XML." www.json.org/xml.html.

Kranen, Hay. "Linked Data and the Semantic Web: GLAM's Betting on the Wrong Horse?" Haykranen.nl. Last modified May 19, 2014. www.haykranen.nl/2014/05/19/linked -data-and-the-semantic-web-glams-betting-on-the-wrong-horse/.

Kroeger, Angela. "The Road to BIBFRAME: The Evolution of the Idea of Bibliographic Transition into a Post-MARC Future." *Cataloging & Classification Quarterly* 51, no. 8 (2013): 873–90. https://doi.org/10.1080/01639374.2013.823584.

Kruk, Sebastian Ryszard, and Bill McDaniel, eds. *Semantic Digital Libraries*. London: Springer, 2009.

LD4L. "LD4L: Linked Data for Libraries." www.ld4l.org/.

Library of Congress. "On the Record: Report of the Library of Congress Working Group on the Future of Bibliographic Control." Last modified January 9, 2008. www.loc.gov/ bibliographic-future/news/lcwg-ontherecord-jan08-final.pdf.

Library of Congress, Bibliographic Framework Initiative. "Bibliographic Framework as a Web of Data: Linked Data Model and Supporting Services." Last modified November 21, 2012. www.loc.gov/bibframe/pdf/marcld-report-11-21-2012.pdf.

———. "Overview of the BIBFRAME 2.0 Model (Bibliographic Framework Initiative)." Last modified April 21, 2016. www.loc.gov/bibframe/docs/bibframe2-model.html.

Library of Congress, Network Development and MARC Standards Office. "020: International Standard Book Number." Last modified September 24, 2013. www.loc .gov/marc/bibliographic/bd020.html.

———. "MARC Discussion Paper No. 2010-DP01." Last modified December 21, 2010. www.loc.gov/marc/marbi/2010/2010-dp01.html.

———. "776: Additional Physical Form Entry." Last modified May 17, 2017. www.loc.gov/ marc/bibliographic/bd776.html.

Lunden, Ingrid. "Amazon's Share of the U.S. E-Commerce Market Is Now 49%, or 5% of All Retail Spend." Techcrunch. Last modified July 13, 2018. https://techcrunch .com/2018/07/13/amazons-share-of-the-us-e-commerce-market-is-now-49-or-5-of -all-retail-spend/.

Marr, Bernard. "What Is a Data Lake? A Super-Simple Explanation for Anyone." *Forbes*. Last modified August 27, 2018. www.forbes.com/sites/bernardmarr/2018/08/27/what -is-a-data-lake-a-super-simple-explanation-for-anyone/.

Meehan, Thomas. "What's Wrong with MARC?" Slideshare. Last modified February 19, 2015. www.slideshare.net/orangeaurochs/whats-wrong-with-marc.

Murphy, Bob. "OCLC Adds Linked Data to WorldCat.org." News Releases, OCLC. Last modified June 20, 2012. https://worldcat.org/arcviewer/7/OCC/2015/03/19/ H1426803137790/viewer/file1303.html.

Musella, Davide. "The META Tag of HTML." IETF Tools. Last updated December 20, 1995. https://tools.ietf.org/html/draft-musella-html-metatag-01.

Naughton, John. *A Brief History of the Future*. London: Weidenfeld & Nicolson, 1999.

OCLC. "Linked Data Survey." www.oclc.org/research/themes/data-science/linkeddata/ linked-data-survey.html.

Open Data Institute. "First ODI Open Data Awards Presented by Sirs Tim Berners-Lee and Nigel Shadbolt." Last modified November 4, 2014. Archived from the original at https://web.archive.org/web/20160324003214/; http://theodi.org/news/first-odi-open-data-awards-presented-by-sir-tim-berners-lee-and-sir-nigel-shadbolt.

Palzer, Daniel. "Ontology-Based Services in Multi-Agent Systems." Diploma thesis, University of Porto, Portugal, 2005. https://web.fe.up.pt/~eol/SOCRATES/Palzer/.

Pattie, Ling Yuh W. "Henriette Davidson Avram, the Great Legacy." *Cataloging & Classification Quarterly* 25, no. 2-3 (1998): 67–81. https://doi.org/10.1300/J104v25n02_05.

PricewaterhouseCoopers. "A New Video World Order: What Motivates Consumers?" www.pwc.com/us/en/services/consulting/library/consumer-intelligence-series/video-consumer-motivations.html.

Ryan, Johnny. *A History of the Internet and the Digital Future.* London: Reaktion, 2010.

Salo, Dorothea. "Quia Faciendum Est." Speaker Deck. Last modified October 23, 2015. https://speakerdeck.com/dsalo/quia-faciendum-est-with-notes.

Schubert, Mark. "RDF Is Not XML: RDF Serialization and iiRDS Metadata." Parson. Last modified December 4, 2018. www.parson-europe.com/de/wissensartikel/557-rdf-is-not-xml-rdf-serialization-and-iirds-metadata.html.

Seikel, Michele, and Thomas Steele. "How MARC Has Changed: The History of the Format and Its Forthcoming Relationship to RDA." *Technical Services Quarterly* 28, no. 3 (2011): 322–34. https://doi.org/10.1080/07317131.2011.574519.

Sollins, K., and L. Masinter. "Functional Requirements for Uniform Resource Names." Network Working Group, IETF Tools. Last modified December 1994. https://tools.ietf.org/html/rfc1737.

Spicher, Karen M. "The Development of the MARC Format." *Cataloging & Classification Quarterly* 21, no. 3-4 (1996): 75–90. https://doi.org/10.1300/J104v21n03_06.

Sporny, Manu. "JSON-LD and Why I Hate the Semantic Web." Manu.Sporny.org. Last modified January 21, 2014. Archived from the original at https://web.archive.org/web/20190405035404/; http://manu.sporny.org/2014/json-ld-origins-2/.

Statista. "Social Media Usage Worldwide." www.statista.com/study/12393/social-networks-statista-dossier/.

Stuart, David. "Library and Information Professionals: Builders of the Ontological Universe." *Information Today.* Last modified January 1, 2014. www.thefree library.com/Library+and+information+professionals%3A+builders +of+the+ontological +...-a0360995275.

Sullivan, Danny. "Meta Keywords Tag 101: How to 'Legally' Hide Words on Your Pages for Search Engines." Search Engine Land. Last modified September 5, 2007. https://searchengineland.com/meta-keywords-tag-101-how-to-legally-hide-words-on-your-pages-for-search-engines-12099.

Tanon, Thomas Pellissier, Denny Vrandečić, Sebastian Schaffert, Thomas Steiner, and Lydia Pintscher. "From Freebase to Wikidata: The Great Migration." *Proceedings of the 25th International Conference on World Wide Web* (2016): 1419–28. https://dl.acm.org/citation.cfm?id=2874809.

Tennis, Joseph T., and Javier Calzada-Prado. "Ontologies and the Semantic Web: Problems and Perspectives for LIS Professionals." *Ibersid* 12 (2007). https://digital.lib.washington.edu/researchworks/handle/1773/37954.

Tillett, Barbara. "What Is FRBR? A Conceptual Model for the Bibliographic Universe." Library of Congress. Originally published in *Technicalities* 25, no. 5 (2003). www.loc.gov/cds/downloads/FRBR.PDF.

Tillman, Ruth Kitchin. "Barriers to Ethical Name Modeling in Current Linked Data Encoding Practices." In *Ethical Questions in Name Authority Control*, ed. Jane Sandberg, 241–57. Sacramento, CA: Library Juice, 2019.

———. "Linked Data Is Made of Systems." Ruthtillman.com. Last modified May 16, 2019. http://ruthtillman.com/linked-data-is-made-of-systems/.

Verborgh, Ruben, and Seth van Hooland. *Linked Data for Libraries, Archives and Museums: How to Clean, Link, and Publish Your Metadata*. London: Facet, 2014.

Verborgh, Ruben, and Miel Vander Sande. "The Semantic Web Identity Crisis: In Search of the Trivialities That Never Were." Ruben.verborgh.org. Last modified May 21, 2019. https://ruben.verborgh.org/articles/the-semantic-web-identity-crisis/.

Wikidata. "Wikidata:Notability." Last modified July 1, 2019. www.wikidata.org/wiki/Wikidata:Notability.

Wikipedia. "Help:Infobox." Last modified October 17, 2018. https://en.wikipedia.org/wiki/Help:Infobox.

———. "MARC Standards." Last modified July 18, 2019. https://en.wikipedia.org/wiki/MARC_standards.

Williams, Tim. "Overcoming Resistance to Technology Change: A Linked Data Perspective." PHUSE EU Connect 2018. www.phusewiki.org/docs/Frankfut%20Connect%202018/TT/Papers/TT01-tt04-19214.pdf.

World Wide Web Consortium. "Extensible Markup Language (XML) 1.0 (Fifth Edition)." Last modified February 7, 2013. www.w3.org/TR/REC-xml/.

———. "HTML+RDFa 1.1: Support for RDFa in HTML4 and HTML5." 2nd ed. Last modified March 17, 2015. www.w3.org/TR/html-rdfa/.

———. "Ontologies." www.w3.org/standards/semanticweb/ontology.

———. "RDF 1.1 Concepts and Abstract Syntax." Last modified February 25, 2014. www.w3.org/TR/rdf11-concepts/.

———. "RDF 1.1 N-Triples: A Line-Based Syntax for an RDF Graph." Last modified February 25, 2014. www.w3.org/TR/n-triples/.

———. "RDF 1.1 Primer." World Wide Web Consortium. Last modified June 24, 2014. www.w3.org/TR/rdf11-primer/.

———. "RDF Schema 1.1." Last modified February 25, 2014. www.w3.org/TR/rdf-schema/.

World Wide Web Consortium, W3C/IETF URI Planning Interest Group. "URIs, URLs, and URNs: Clarifications and Recommendations 1.0." Last modified September 21, 2001. www.w3.org/TR/uri-clarification/.

GLOSSARY

BIBFRAME: A library-focused linked data format intended to replace MARC. An upper-level linked data ontology, it uniquely identifies entities and concepts found in bibliographic data and exposes the relationships within that data through RDF.

Class: An ontology component that represents a category of shared, general qualities to which other classes or individuals belong. Examples of classes in our hypothetical linked dataset are *Humans, Bands, and Musical Albums.*

Data model: A description of data organization. When abstracted, this is often referred to as a *conceptual data model.* Data models are often expressed in diagrams.

Data reconciliation: *See* **Reconciliation.**

Datatype: In the context of an RDF graph, each literal has an associated datatype to ensure the literal value is absolutely clear. For example, the *date-time* datatype explicitly identifies a string like '1975-12-15' as representing a point in time.

GLAM: Galleries, libraries, archives, and museums.

Graph: In the context of linked data, a collection of RDF statements.

Graph database: A type of database designed to store graph data.

Hypertext Markup Language (HTML): The standard markup language for documents connected through the World Wide Web.

Indexing (search engine): The process of crawling and compiling web data so it can be queried.

Individual: An ontology component representing a single, discrete entity (as opposed to a class). For example, the band Parliament would be an individual example of the class *Musical Group.* (*See also* **Node.**)

Inferencing: In the context of semantic data, drawing conclusions from linked data through computer processing.

Linked data: Technologies and principles—including the use of structured data and unique identifiers to represent knowledge and resources—that, when used together, create machine-readable, extensible data that can be leveraged to expose and create relationships between datasets.

Literal: Information about a node expressed as a label, as opposed to information about a node represented by another node. Literals are typically strings of text or numbers. They may be tagged with a particular datatype to clarify the value of the literal.

MARC: The long-standing library bibliographic format, short for *Machine-Readable Cataloging.*

Metadata Application Profile (MAP): Sets of metadata elements, policies, and guidelines that may or may not be drawn from existing metadata schemas and standards, defined for a particular institutional or domain application.

Minting: Creating and publishing URIs on the web to represent data.

Namespace: Often declared at the beginning of an RDF document, a namespace indicates which linked data vocabularies or ontologies are used within the document's RDF statements.

Node: A specific, unambiguous thing in a dataset. Nodes appear in semantic data under two broad types: *Classes and Individuals.*

Object: The third component of an RDF triple statement, an entity (or literal) that is acted upon by the triple subject.

Ontology: An abstract model representing some domain of knowledge. In linked data, ontologies take the form of specifications (rules) that deal with concepts (information) in a formal (standard) and shared (community-accepted) way.

Parsing: A mechanized function that separates data into discrete parts for processing, usually by a computer script or program.

Predicate: The second component of an RDF triple that represents a relationship connection between the subject and the object.

Property: *See* **Predicate.**

Reconciliation: The process of identifying unique identities in a dataset and matching those with identical entities in another dataset. This often involves adding the URIs of matching entities to a dataset.

Resource Description Framework (RDF): A collection of W3C specifications that create a general method for describing information through web resources.

Semantic triple: *See* Triple.

Semantic Web: The theoretical framework in which web data is packaged in a way that can be understood by machines—computers, bots, and other automated processors—as well as by humans.

Serialization: The process by which data is converted to a different format without losing the original, underlying structure. Common serializations for RDF data are RDF/XML, N-Triples, Turtle, and JSON-LD.

SPARQL: Pronounced "sparkle," a query language and a protocol for traversing RDF data. It can be used to execute complex RDF queries over multiple graphs, validate the structure of a graph, and even add new triples to existing RDF data. (The term is a recursive acronym for *SPARQL Protocol* and *RDF Query Language.*)

Subclass: An ontology component that shares the characteristics of a particular class, but represents a subset of that broader class. The individuals in a subclass will have all of the characteristics in common with the broader class, and the subclass to which they belong, but may not have the characteristics of a different subclass.

Subject: The first component of an RDF triple statement, representing the concept or thing about which the RDF statement is made.

"Things, not strings": A phrase often used in linked data discussions, representing a shift away from text-based identifiers, or labels, to *things*, entities represented by URIs and containing RDF underneath.

Triple: A statement made in RDF comprised of three parts: a *subject*, a *predicate*, and an *object*, in that order. The Subject-Predicate-Object components of RDF triples are the atomic-level particles of semantic data.

Triple statement: *See* **Triple.**

Triplestore: A kind of graph database designed to store semantic data. It gets its name from the statements made in RDF called *triples*.

Uniform Resource Locator (URL): A web resource that specifies its location on a computer network. It is a specific type of URI; the combination of a location and a mechanism for retrieving it (*http, ftp, mailto, etc.*) turns a URI into a URL.

Universal Resource Identifier (URI): An identifier that describes either a web resource's location, its name, or both. Being locators as well as identifiers makes URIs integral to linked data and the Semantic Web.

World Wide Web: An information system in which resources are interlinked and accessible over the internet.

World Wide Web Consortium (W3C): An international standards organization that develops and approves specifications for the World Wide Web.

FIGURE CREDITS

Figure 1.1: Tim Berners-Lee photo © ITU Pictures, licensed under CC BY 2.0 (https://creativecommons.org/licenses/by/2.0/). Cropped from the original, via Flickr [www.flickr.com/photos/itupictures/16662336315].

Figure 1.2: Charlie Chaplin photo by P. D. Jankens, via Wikimedia [https://commons.wikimedia.org/wiki/File:Charlie_Chaplin.jpg]. Douglas Fairbanks photograph by Harris & Ewing, courtesy of the Library of Congress, Prints & Photographs Division, LC-DIG-hec-16616, [www.loc.gov/pictures/item/2016857680/]. Mary Pickford photo courtesy of the Library of Congress, Prints & Photographs Division, LC-USZ62-113150 [www.loc.gov/pictures/item/95502963/]. United Artists founding photo courtesy of the Library of Congress, Prints & Photographs Division, LC-USZ62-137195 [http://www.loc.gov/pictures/item/2007678308/]. *Mark of Zorro* poster via Wikimedia [https://commons.wikimedia.org/wiki/File:FairbanksMarkofZorro.jpg]. *Gold Rush* poster via Wikimedia [https://commons.wikimedia.org/wiki/File:Gold_rush_poster.jpg]. *Dorothy Vernon of Haddon Hall* poster via Wikimedia [https://commons.wikimedia.org/wiki/File:Dorothy_Vernon_of_Haddon_Hall_-_film_poster.jpg].

Figure 2.1: George Clinton photo © Joe Van, licensed under CC BY 2.0 (https://creativecommons.org/licenses/by/2.0/), via Flickr [www.flickr.com/photos/glowjangles/4081046882/].

Figure 3.2: George Clinton photo © Flickr user "snabby," licensed under Creative Commons CC BY 2.0 (https://creativecommons.org/licenses/by/2.0/), cropped from the original, via Flickr [www.flickr.com/photos/snabby/3757260364/].

Figure 5.7 inspired by a diagram at DBpedia, https://wiki.dbpedia.org/about.

Figure 5.8: Linked Open Data Cloud visualization images courtesy of http://lod-cloud.net, licensed under CC BY 4.0 (https://creativecommons.org/licenses/by-sa/4.0/).

Figures 5.9 & 5.10: Bootsy Collins photo © Mikael Väisänen, under Creative Commons CC BY-SA (https://creativecommons.org/licenses/by-sa/4.0/), cropped from the original, via Wikimedia [https://commons.wikimedia.org/wiki/File:William_%E2%80%9EBootsy%E2%80%9C_Collins.jpg].

Figure 6.1: George Clinton photo © Joseph Schneid, licensed under Creative Commons CC BY 3.0 (https://creativecommons.org/licenses/by/3.0/), cropped from the original, via Wikimedia [https://en.wikipedia.org/wiki/File:George_Clinton_%26_Parliament_Funkadelic_performing_in_Waterfront_Park,_Louisville,_Kentucky_on_July_4th,_2008.jpg].

ABOUT THE AUTHORS

SCOTT CARLSON is a library software developer for Arizona State University. Previously, he was metadata coordinator at Rice University's Fondren Library and cataloging and metadata librarian at the American University of Sharjah (in the United Arab Emirates). His favorite P-Funk albums are *Maggot Brain*, *Mothership Connection*, and *Free Your Mind . . . and Your Ass Will Follow*, in that order.

CORY LAMPERT is a professor and the head of digital collections at the University of Nevada, Las Vegas. She is responsible for the strategy and management of digital initiatives for the University Libraries' Special Collections and Archives. Her research interests include implementing linked open data for digital collections, with a focus on empowering librarians to learn through practice. She is active in grant-writing, building collaborative digitization and community engagement partnerships, and mentoring new professionals. Lampert received a BA in liberal arts from Sarah Lawrence College and an MLIS from the University of Wisconsin-Milwaukee. Her favorite P-Funk albums include the well-worn *Mothership Connection* LP that she bought on a New York City street corner in '93 and her *Maggot Brain/Funkadelic* playlist, though she feels there is no substitute for live funk music.

DARNELLE MELVIN is the special collections and archives metadata librarian and an assistant professor at the University of Nevada, Las Vegas, where he is responsible for managing metadata activities, remediation projects, and metadata documentation. He researches metadata and resource discovery in relation to digital libraries, repository migrations, and data warehousing. His work explores linked data implementation, metadata remediation tools/services, workflow engineering and optimization, and semantic and syntactic interoperability. Melvin received his MLIS degree from San José State University and his BA from San Francisco State University. His favorite P-Funk album is *The Clones of Dr. Funkenstein*.

ANNE WASHINGTON is the metadata services coordinator at the University of Houston Libraries, where she is responsible for managing metadata creation and maintenance for the University of Houston digital collections and other repository services. Her research interests include technologies, such as linked data, that have the potential to more broadly expose and connect resources, as well as inclusive, user-centered approaches to metadata. She received her MLIS degree from the University of Wisconsin-Milwaukee. Her favorite P-Funk albums are *Mothership Connection* and *Chocolate City*.

INDEX